NATIONAL PARK MYSTERIES & DISAPPEARANCES

THE GREAT SMOKY MOUNTAINS NATIONAL PARK

STEVE STOCKTON

BEYOND THE FRAY
Publishing

ISBN 13: 978-1-954528-06-2

Beyond The Fray Publishing, a division of Beyond The Fray, LLC, San Diego, CA
www.beyondthefraypublishing.com

BEYOND THE FRAY

Publishing

INTRODUCTION

The Great Smoky Mountains National Park and surrounding areas (to include Gatlinburg, Pigeon Forge, Townsend, Wears Valley [Tennessee side], and Cherokee and surrounds [North Carolina side]) have always held a special place in my heart. Having been born and raised in East Tennessee, I was usually within an hour's drive to the area for the first forty years of my life. Many, many times, we would decide on a whim to take a weekend in the mountains, get away from the hustle and bustle of West Knoxville or Oak Ridge, someplace to get away for a few days and relax in the bucolic mountains, with its crisp air, mountain streams and other flora and fauna associated therewith.

As a child, we would often go on family vacations to Gatlinburg, along with my brother and his family, making for many truly wonderful and fun memories. I learned to swim during the two weeks we spent at the Glenstone Lodge one summer. My nephew and I locked all the keys in one of the two adjoining rooms we were sharing at the Ramada Inn on the Parkway (the high-rise building in the back), which saw employees climbing across the balconies several stories up to get us back into the room.

We also got into a lot of mischief, such as the time we sent two elderly female "leaf lookers" (people who come into the mountains in the fall to view the beautiful foliage) on a wild-goose chase to catch the "Comanche Train" (an electric conveyance similar to an extended golf cart that hauled tourists all over Gatlinburg proper, prior to the city installing the Mountain Trolley mass transit)... I could go on and on—perhaps I'll write a book of our youthful misadventures someday (although I probably need to check what the statute of limitations are regarding some of our shenanigans)!

The Smokies are not only a popular destination for the tourist and vacationer, but are a popular destination for honeymooners as well—yours truly stayed in Gatlinburg after my first marriage. On any given weekend, especially in the spring and summer, the number of newlyweds staying in Gatlinburg (and neighboring Pigeon Forge, for the shop-happy and budget conscious, or the Wears Valley and Townsend areas for those truly wanting privacy and lack of crowds) can easily be in the thousands.

But aside from all that, far and away from the flora and fauna and funnel cakes, there's a dark side to the Smokies and surrounding foothills. A very dark side— mysteries abound: myths, murders, mayhem and missing people, vanished without a trace. Bloodthirsty murders. Bone-chilling paranormal hauntings and ghost sightings.

So put aside your mountain corndogs, your guide-books to trees and bears and nature, park your RV and your Rascal scooters—forget about the pretty leaves, the relaxing stream as well as the miniature golf, the funnel cakes and all the other "tourist traps," and prepare for a wild ride on the dark side of the Great Smoky Mountains.

PART 1

HAUNTINGS

CHAPTER ONE

LYDIA, THE LONESOME GHOST OF THE GREENBRIER LODGE

IN THE 1930S, the Greenbrier Lodge catered exclusively to wealthy travelers—hunters and tourists alike—from all over the Southeast.

The legend goes that, back in the day, a young woman named Lydia was staying at the Greenbrier Lodge for an extended visit. A beautiful young girl, Lydia was absolutely head over heels in love with a young gentleman from nearby, and they were engaged to be wed one fine day in the mountains. When her wedding day came, the beautiful Lydia went to the church, resplendent in her beautiful white gown, and waited at the altar for her betrothed. She was so excited —ah, to be young and totally in love and about to be wed to the one with whom you are prepared to spend the rest of your life!

Unfortunately, Lydia's husband-to-be came down with a devilish case of the proverbial "cold feet." As the church bells tolled, the scheduled hour of the wedding came and went, and poor, beautiful Lydia finally came to the conclusion that she had been stood up by her fiancé, left alone at the altar—possibly the worst and most embarrassing thing that could happen to any lovely young lady. As one would expect, Lydia was devastated.

Although she had waited several hours at the church —quite a time beyond when she was already sure she was going to be stood up by her husband-to-be, Lydia eventually conceded defeat and returned to the Greenbrier Lodge.

Shortly after her return to the lodge, she tried but failed to convince herself that everything was going to be all right. After all, she reasoned, it wasn't like she was the first (nor would she be the last) bride to be jilted on her wedding day.

But the more Lydia thought about the prospect of returning to her home and her family and her neighbors (oh, how their tongues would set to wagging!) and the questions and blame and whispers and giggling that would inevitably follow her for the rest of her life, Lydia glumly decided that she had no life left to live. She made up her mind how she would handle the problem at hand. She knew there was no turning back now; she was in too deep, too far—there was no way she would return home a forlorn mess, a shadow of her formal beautiful self.

Sadly, the Greenbrier Lodge staff found Lydia early the next morning, hanging from the rafter beam, a length of rope laced around her neck. Oddly enough, in the days following the untimely death of Lydia, the body of her husband-to-be was found elsewhere in the Great Smoky Mountains National Park—as it turns out, he had not left her at the altar intentionally at all—he had met his own death as a result of a mountain lion attack while hunting small game. Please note, however, that there is an alternate version of the tale that has Lydia's fiancé being killed *after* she was abandoned at the altar and took her own life—the locals who believed this version were the ones who claimed Lydia had returned in spirit in the form of a large mountain cat to seek her revenge.

Regardless of the backstory that you believe, it was shortly after the tragic, needless suicide of Lydia that her spirit was said to have begun haunting the Greenbrier Lodge—when one so young and so beautiful takes their life with their own hand over what turned out to be a misunderstanding and a separate tragedy in its own right, it would be more surprising if a haunting *didn't* result.

Due to the nature of her death, the superstitious mountain folk initially buried Lydia in an unmarked grave, feeling it would be bad luck to give a person who had committed suicide a "proper Christian burial" in a churchyard or cemetery. This did not bode well with the restless spirit of Lydia, who was said to have kept a certain caretaker at the lodge awake at night with the haunting plea of "mark my grave, mark my grave." After a few sleepless nights of being awakened by the pleading ghost, the caretaker reached the conclusion that he'd had enough. Knowing where Lydia was buried, he strode off in the dark of night to a spot in the deep woods below the lodge and erected a simple marker at the grave. This seemed to have given the ghost at least some measure of comfort, as the caretaker was able to sleep that night— and all subsequent nights—through afterwards.

Nowadays, after a few different owners and incarnations, the Greenbrier Lodge has been rechristened the Greenbrier Restaurant, an upscale family dinner destination in the East Gatlinburg area off of Highway 321, near the Dudley Creek area. It is said that the ghost of Lydia is still active at the location, and is most often seen on the stairs near the second-floor landing. Other guests have seen her manifest in the form of a petite, sad girl who is there one second and gone the next.

The serving staff as well as the current proprietors of the Greenbrier Restaurant admit that they, too, sometimes feel the chilling presence of young Lydia. Kitchen workers also state that sometimes food items will fly off the shelves in the kitchen, or cooking implements such as ladles and spoons left in one area will sometimes inexplicably turn up in another area. Perhaps the ghost is upset due to the menu item that bears her namesake—"Lydia's Chocolate Suicide For Two," which states that it is "simply to die for" (here's a gastronomic hint from your ol' buddy Steve: if you do go to the Greenbrier, try the French onion soup—it is out of this world [ha-ha] and might be the best you have ever had).

The Greenbrier Restaurant is located at 370 Newman Road, Gatlinburg, TN 37738, and please note that they do NOT accept reservations—first come, first served, so get there early if you want to make sure you get a seat. The restaurant is open Sunday–Thursday 4:30 p.m.–9:00 p.m. and on Friday & Saturday 4:30 p.m.–10:00 p.m. Their telephone number is (865) 436-6318, and you can check out their website at http://www.greenbrierrestaurant.com. If you do visit, don't be shy about asking about Lydia—the staff and owners LOVE to talk about their resident ghost.

CHAPTER TWO

THE HAUNTING OF THE EDGEWATER HOTEL

RIVER ROAD IN GATLINBURG, which runs parallel to the Parkway, but a block or so farther over, has a few spooky areas. One of these is Gatlinburg's Mysterious Mansion, a haunted attraction built in the early 1980s. It's a really amazing representation of a typical haunted house, with a self-guided tour that includes hidden stairways, collapsing balconies, secret passages (look behind the grandfather clock!), paintings with eyes that move, and a few surprises that leap out at you from the darkest corners of the attraction. It's all in good fun, and everyone except perhaps the very smallest of children will enjoy the frights inside.

However, just a little ways up River Road from the Mysterious Mansion is the site of a real haunting...

The Edgewater Hotel is so named because it is just

that—it sits on the very edge of the Cliff Branch, a rushing mountain stream that runs through Gatlinburg on that side of town. In fact, you even have to drive across a little bridge over the fast-flowing branch to get to the hotel's parking area. Situated right over the rushing water, each room's balcony has a lovely view of the mountains in the distance and the sight and sound of the swiftly flowing water below, a full eight stories from the top of the hotel.

It was here from one of these very balconies that a little girl, perhaps leaning out too far to get a good look at the water below, fell to her death in the 1980s. Reports at the time are vague on the events surrounding the tragedy, and the city of Gatlinburg like for people to only have a good time when visiting—tourism is Gatlinburg's number one industry.

Much like the Disney Magic Kingdom in Florida (where critically and mortally injured patrons are taken across to the street to the hospital in the town of Celebration to be pronounced dead—this way they can sort of truthfully make the claim that no one has "died" in the Magic Kingdom, although that's not exactly true), Gatlinburg wants to keep things like murders and suicides and children falling to their deaths from hotel balconies on the quiet and down-low. Again, the tourism dollar of Gatlinburg and of the Great Smoky Mountains

National Park (the most-visited national park in the United States, with visitors easily numbering over the million mark every year) is the name of the game.

So, for whatever reason and under whatever circumstances, a young girl, approximately five years of age, plunged to her death from one of the upper balconies at the Edgewater Hotel. It's said she was up before her parents, either early in the morning or very late at night, depending on the version you hear from the locals—she wasn't found until her parents noticed her missing at a later time, and they rushed to the balcony only to see her small, lifeless body on a rock in the rushing waters below the hotel.

Now, it's said that on the anniversary of her death, the figure of a child can be spotted on a balcony of the hotel's upper floors. Just as the child falls, the image fades and is no longer visible. It's also been said that the spirit of the little girl has also been spotted on the rock in the river where she died, forlornly looking up and perhaps even pointing to the balcony from where she fell.

As you might have gathered, the hotel is not exactly falling over themselves to discuss this incident, and many of the employees of the hotel will simply deny any knowledge of what you're talking about. Your best bet would be to ask friendly locals over the age of forty, who will most likely not only remember the event and be willing to talk about it, but may have sightings of their own.

The Edgewater Hotel is located at 402 River Rd, Gatlinburg, TN 37738. Their phone number is (865) 436-4151, and their website can be accessed at http://edgewater-hotel.com. Again, I must stress that if you wish to investigate here, do it as legally and as non invasively as possible. Consider getting a room unless you just want to look from the sidewalk on the other side of the water from the very busy hotel. Otherwise, it's considered trespassing.

CHAPTER THREE

THE HAUNTING OF WHEATLANDS PLANTATION

ACCORDING TO AN ARTICLE ONLINE, "There have been more than seventy murders and deaths in the house, and the battles of the Revolutionary and the Civil Wars were fought on the grounds." Did that get your attention? Well, it should—if you're looking for a grade A, number 1, sure-fire, certified haunted location around the Smoky Mountain area, then the Wheatland Plantation in nearby Sevierville, Tennessee, should fit the bill nicely.

Located just off the Boyd's Creek Highway area in Sevierville, Wheatland Plantation is a family farm built around an 1820 Federal-style plantation home, the exact construction spot of which was chosen by the existence of a large geode(!) that can still be seen in the basement of the mansion. Perhaps the crystals inside this giant stone have created an energy vortex that has drawn so much death and violence and destruction to an otherwise bucolic country setting in the foothills of the Great Smoky Mountains.

In addition to the incredibly large death tally from inside the house, the immediate grounds are hardly a Sunday school picnic, either. It is known that over two dozen Cherokee braves were slaughtered in the Battle of Boyd's Creek, the creek which still runs adjacent to the main property. The mortal remains of these fallen Indian warriors are said to be buried in a mass grave in the woods behind the house, where legend has it that "the bodies were stacked like cordwood," which makes the spirits of the braves restless, naturally.

In addition to the Cherokee mass grave, there are also the graves of seventy or so former plantation slaves of African American descent. And the bodies of two Revolutionary War soldiers, evidently so that no one group felt left out.

The Wheatlands, so named due to the large crop of wheat harvested year after year, was started and intended to remain a family farming enterprise by the Chandler family. The farm was originally intended to be left to Revolutionary War veteran Timothy Chandler; however Chandler's mother (and the matriarch of the Chandler clan) thought that dear Timothy had too much of a taste for alcohol, and instead left the family farm to her grandson, John Chandler (Timothy Chandler's son), in 1819, and under the grandson's steady hand and forward vision, the plantation prospered so well as to eventually become one of Sevier County's largest farms, covering 3,700 acres by the mid-1800s. After the Civil War, John Chandler bequeathed parcels of Wheatlands to some of the plantation's now-free slaves in 1875. These freed peoples also helped found the area to the south of the plantation, now known as the Chandler Gap community. It was said that John Chandler treated his slaves so fairly that even after they were freed, the majority chose to remain on or near the plantation, which prompted Chandler's outpouring of heartfelt generosity with his family's land.

As previously mentioned, Timothy was denied his birthright due to his love of strong drink, and when his son John inherited the property from Grandma Chandler, it didn't sit well with Timothy—a silent, brooding rage began to build inside the aging military veteran. Eventually hurt feelings and words of anger turned into threats and physical altercations. During a particularly vicious attack by Timothy, John was defending himself with a fireplace poker and (allegedly) accidentally killed his father by using the iron poker to hit (or stab, depending on the tale you hear) the old man a wee bit too hard, just below the ribs. Timothy doubled over in pain, bleeding profusely and, no longer willing to fight, retired to his quarters, where he died as a result of his injuries, most likely due to internal injuries, blood loss, and shock.

On the floor of the plantation house, the bloodstains left by Timothy Chandler during this final altercation can still be seen in the parlor. Over the decades, many attempts have been made to scrub the bloodstains from the wooden floor, but they always continue to return— some have said even more tenaciously than before with each new occurrence. It has been reported that the sanding down of the boards by an experienced floor care professional did not keep the stains from coming back in a relatively short time. There have been many teams of paranormal investigators tour the Wheatlands, and they all seem to be drawn to the dark spots on the floor of the parlor where the beginning of the end occurred for Timothy Chandler, as if his very blood cries out from the floor.

As far as paranormal activity goes, the house and grounds are considered to be *very* active. Ghostly apparitions, ethereal moans, disembodied voices, phantom gunshots and more have been reported at this location. Sometimes faces are seen in the windows when the plantation house is supposed to be empty, and what appears to be the flickering of candlelight has also been reported inside after hours. The Wheatland Plantation regularly offers ghost night tours, and the entire site can be rented out by paranormal groups desiring to investigate this hotbed of the supernatural.

Wheatlands Plantation is located at 2507 Boyd's Creek Hwy, Sevierville, TN. Tours of the house and grounds are offered regularly, as well as the occasional paranormal investigation or similar event. For more information, please call (865) 365-1052 during regular business hours. The site also maintains a web presence at http://wheatlandsplantation.org, which contains much additional information, history, and photographs.

CHAPTER FOUR

THE ROCKY TOP VILLAGE INN MURDERS & HAUNTING

ONE EXAMPLE that springs readily to mind regarding a "residual haunting" is the Rocky Top Village Inn motel haunting in Gatlinburg, Tennessee. The inn, famous for being the place where Felice and Boudreaux Bryant penned the famous song for which the motel is named (they also wrote most of the Everly Brothers hits and have had some of their other songs covered by a diverse array of artists, including Nazareth, Joan Jett, Bob Dylan and the Beach boys), is also the site of a brutal double murder.

The grisly deaths, dubbed "the Rocky Top Murders" by the local press, happened in 1986. Security guard Troy Valentine, thirty-six, and night clerk Melissa Hill, twenty-one, were horrifically stabbed and shot to death in the tiny motel back office on the night of September

13, 1986, and their bodies (which weren't immediately found) were stashed in room #1 of this otherwise quiet mountain retreat that still to this day looks like it was transported wholesale from the early 1970s. Apparently the motive was robbery, although the take was only $413 and whatever cash Hill had in her purse. Four men, including the notorious local maniac known as "Tattoo Eddie," were arrested for the crime. Eddie was sentenced to death, but this was later commuted to a life sentence (like the other three perpetrators) when it was discovered Eddie has an IQ of 70 (which, in Tennessee, prevents an inmate from being put to death). Although his life was spared and he would never breathe the air a free man, perhaps justice eventually caught up with Eddie—he was found murdered in his cell (brutally stabbed to death with a homemade "shank") on March 10, 2015. It's a possibility that his ghost now wanders the rows of cells of the Morgan County Correctional Facility, in Wartburg, Tennessee.

But back to the haunting at the motel.

According to Gatlinburg locals, the motel has never been the same since the murders (unsurprisingly so, as brutal murders tend to not bode well in resort towns). This author concurs. When I last visited the motel, during part of a paranormal investigation in the early 2000s, I found the residual energy to be quite palpable.

And although I am very "in tune" to such energies and have been able to detect them since childhood, some of the other investigators on this outing weren't as psychically "sensitive," yet they felt it as well. There is a heaviness that permeates the very air around the Rocky Top Village Inn. Oddly enough, there are other haunted motels not just in Gatlinburg, but on the very same stretch of Historic Nature Trail Road where the Rocky Top Village Inn is located (another entry in this book).

The majority of reports are centered around the tiny motel office where the murders occurred. The "office" is tiny because it is actually a satellite office at the back of the hotel on Reagan Road, meant for convenient check-in/out during regular business hours. It's truly not much bigger than a walk-in closet. The motel property owners have a nice, big "normal" office for their needs on the other side of the complex fronting on Historic Nature Trail Road (formerly Airport Road). In fact, that was why the bodies were discovered—when Hill never showed up with the day's deposits at the front office, Valentine was dispatched to check on her, only to share the same twisted fate.

It's expected that the office, as well as room #1 (where the killers stashed the bodies. The rooms have been renumbered, but it's the room adjoining the small office) would have haunting energy. It's said that at night, screams and pleas for mercy can still be heard echoing through the otherwise eerily quiet complex. Just standing in the parking lot outside the office and room is a very unnerving experience and will literally make the hairs on your neck stand up on a dark, quiet night when you imagine the horrors that once befell the innocent just inside those very doors.

The strangest aspect of the haunting for me, though, is the reports concerning the motel's courtyard fountain. Apparently, at some point Hill briefly escaped her attackers, only to be recaptured outside by the ornate water feature. Several people have reported seeing a woman's disembodied legs, only appearing from the knees down, race around near the fountain while screams and moans are heard. Legs only visible from the knees down. I'll let you ponder how truly frightening that would be for a moment.

Now, even as frightening as it would be to see a phantom, there is something even more unsettling (at least to me) about seeing a partial phantom. Full-body ghost? I'll stick around and check that out... Nothing but a pair of legs running around a fountain in the dark? Noooo, thank you!

As expected, the people in the area are still sensitive about the murders. If you wish to visit here, I recommend keeping quiet about the true nature of your visit.

As of this writing (August 2020) the hotel is no longer open for business; however this might be the best time for those interested in doing an investigation. Based on the mercurial nature of businesses in Gatlinburg, I doubt this motel complex will remain closed for long.

The hotel's address is listed as 311 Historic Nature Trail, Gatlinburg, TN 37738; however the allegedly haunted area is on Reagan Road, the street directly behind the motel (if facing the front). You'll know you're in the right area by the infamous fountain in the back office parking area.

CHAPTER FIVE

THE HOLIDAY INN HOLIDOME SUNSPREE RESORT MURDERS

FORMERLY LOCATED next door to the Glenstone Lodge on Historic Natural Trail Road (which was known as Airport Road until recently), the Holiday Inn Holidome SunSpree Resort was a large, rambling structure and very different from the homogenized, two-story look of the myriad cookie-cutter Holiday Inns spread throughout the country. The Gatlinburg version of the resort was multistoried, had a wonderful indoor pool and recreation center (the Holidome) as well as a restaurant, bar and nightclub, complete with a house band blasting out Top-40 hits (I spent a few nights here on many occasions after graduating from high school in nearby Knoxville). I have spent a multitude of nights next door at the Glenstone Lodge (I even learned to swim there as a child, during a two-week summer stay with my family).

While there were always good times to be had at the Glenstone, the real action was always next door in the nightclub of the Holiday Inn.

However, in 1986, the fun at the Holiday Inn took an extraordinarily dark turn—a double murder put a damper on the Holiday Inn SunSpree Resort.

Only those immediately and intimately involved know the complete details of what happened on that night, but for whatever the reason, the outcome remains the same—two teenage girls from neighboring Kentucky were dead, and a bouncer from a local bar was facing the charge of double murder.

The girls, Jenny Stevens and Tonya Roberts, were both from Crestwood, Kentucky, and had been visiting Tanya's grandmother before deciding to stop and spend the night in Gatlinburg. The girls checked in to room 413 on the day of July 29, 1980. Despite the many rumors that have since swirled around this infamous, fateful event, the girls were *not* runaways as had been erroneously reported—they had parental permission both for the trip to visit Tanya's grandmother and for the stay in Gatlinburg.

There is some confusion as to where they met the man who would be charged with their murder, Allen Wayne Hughes—there are stories that he was a bouncer at a bar in downtown Gatlinburg, and the girls met him at the bar while having a drink. I rather doubt this story, as even though the drinking age in Tennessee at the time was eighteen, the girls were aged seventeen and sixteen. I'm sure it's not out of the realm of possibility that the doorman and/or bartender were not checking pretty females' IDs that night—stranger things have happened, I suppose. But for whatever reason, the girls did, indeed, invite Hughes back to their room at the Holiday Inn.

Again, no one knows the details, but apparently Hughes strangled one of the girls in the room while the other girl was in the bathroom, and was attempting to stuff her body under the bed when the other girl emerged. The girl ran out the door and fled for her life, but Hughes caught up to her near a locked door in the stairwell and strangled her to death as well.

The reports of hauntings began almost immediately. The housekeepers at the Holiday Inn soon began to circulate stories of room 413 amongst themselves. Things would be moved around, even if no one had stayed in the room for days (particularly in the off season, this *can* happen). A mirror once shattered for no reason while a maid was dusting in the room. Many employees of the hotel would report sounds coming from the room when it was vacant, including whispers, moans and screams. Apparitions were also spotted outside the room and in the stairwell where the other girl was strangled. Eventually, the management of the hotel had had enough, and removed the room number and decommissioned the room from service. I'm sure the clerks would snicker later on when would-be ghost hunters would specifically request room 413, not knowing they were not staying in the original murder room.

There are, believe it or not, other stories about the Holiday Inn in Gatlinburg as well—one involves a Scoutmaster who was responsible for a young Boy Scout dying on an outing. Although the Boy Scout died elsewhere, the Scoutmaster checked into the Holiday Inn—and then permanently checked himself out—in room 471. Oddly enough, he left a tip of $3.57 for the maid, perhaps to make up for the mess—he shot himself in the head with a .357-caliber pistol. The story is also told that this was a businessman who was denied access to the pool, hence the decision to commit suicide. There is also a twist on the tale that the entire seventh floor of the Holidome Tower was rented to the Boy Scouts, and the aforementioned Scoutmaster killed several of the Scouts in his charge before killing himself.

Out behind the hotel, there was a family-style/smorgasbord restaurant where it's rumored that a cook named Alvin died or was killed or killed himself. However poor Alvin left the planet (and from where), his ghost is active at the banquet room in the back of the complex. Other restaurant workers report hearing voices, seeing things thrown around, and finding things in places other than where they were originally left.

Sadly, as of this writing (2020), the Holiday Inn is no more. It changed hands several times after all the tragic incidents and was most recently known as the Garden Plaza hotel. Now, if you look up the address (520 Historic Nature Trail Road Gatlinburg, TN 37738), you are met with a view of the parking lot—the hotel is completely demolished and gone. It appears that the banquet kitchen (the home of the ghost of Alvin the cook) is/was still standing when the Google Maps photo was taken. Is the property, now a vacant lot, still haunted? Who knows, but I think it would be an interesting place for a ghost hunt, especially near the creek and the wooded area at the back of the lot—HOWEVER—I'm sure the vacant lot is still private property—please get permission from the current owner before attempting any visit or investigation. Please be aware that the newer Holiday Inn Club Vacations Gatlinburg-Smoky Mountain Resort (located down the street at 404 Historic Nature Trail, Gatlinburg, TN 37738) is NOT the same hotel as the haunted one, and asking about the murders and hauntings will just make the employees of this VERY DIFFERENT hotel angry.

CHAPTER SIX

WHITE OAK FLATS CEMETERY

NESTLED up above Gatlinburg on a small rise, right behind the haunted attraction and the mini golf course, lies White Oak Flats Cemetery. In fact, Gatlinburg used to be called White Oak Flats.

The White Oak Flats Cemetery, eerie even in broad daylight, let alone in the dark of night, is sort of a hidden-in-plain-sight, road-less-traveled type haunted place in Gatlinburg, Tennessee. Although the cemetery is literally just a few yards from the tourist throngs crowding the sidewalk along the Parkway, it would be easy to overlook the cemetery—as many thousands of people no doubt have over the fifty to sixty or so years so Gatlinburg evolved from a sleepy little mountain town into a world-class vacation destination known for its year-round activities. Basically, if you climb the small hill sort of behind Gatlinburg's shopping center known as the Village, you'll find yourself staring at one of the oldest cemeteries in the Great Smoky Mountains area.

Established in 1830, this hilltop graveyard and cemetery contains the mortal remains of several of White Oak Flats' (aka Gatlinburg) early settling families, such as the Ogles (who more or less started the town and influenced the entire area, including nearby areas, such as Pittman, Pigeon Forge, Cosby, Townsend and Cades Cove) in what appears to be a few eerie, unmarked graves. There's no telling what spooky sights and wandering spirits might walk here on the hill above this mountain town when the sky is dark and the moon is hidden behind the clouds. Come during the day for the history lesson; come back at night, according to local tales and legends, for some haunting activity. As always, be respectful in this (or any) cemetery. The relatives of many folks buried here still live and work in Gatlinburg.

Some of the reported sightings here include hazy white shapes seen flitting among the tombstones, shadow people, a ghostly woman in white, a man dressed as a "cowboy," and at least two different ghost dogs. There are also reports of the eerie sounds of disembodied weeping, moaning, and wailing emanating from the cemetery between the hours of midnight and 2 a.m.

CHAPTER SEVEN

THE LEGEND (AND GHOST) OF BLOWING ROCK

BLOWING ROCK, North Carolina, has a unique version of a not-so-unique legend attached to it. There are many, many "Lover's Leap" type areas throughout not only the south but the entire country and throughout the world—but Blowing Rock puts a decidedly Appalachian spin on the old saw of the tragic, star-crossed lovers who can't be together yet can't be apart, even in death.

There are several scientific explanations for the phenomena, but everyone loves a good ghost story—it was said that a Cherokee brave was in love with a Chickasaw maiden. Since their differing tribes forbade their love, the brave flung himself off the rock one night as the lovers stood contemplating the expanse before them. The winds gusted, picked up the brave, and lofted him back up, into the waiting arms of his Chickasaw lover. They took this as a sign and married despite the union not being accepted by their respective tribes. Legend has it that on certain nights in the summer and fall, the shadow of a brave can be seen leaping from the rock.

While I've never witnessed the apparition, I have seen unusual weather here, with both rain and snow moving *upwards* due to the strong draft. It's also possible when the wind is just right to toss leaves or flowers over the edge of the precipice, only to have them fly back up and out of sight above your head. As always, take caution due to the sheer rock faces and wildly shifting winds when in the area, and obey all warning signs—they are there for your protection.

CHAPTER EIGHT

HAUNTED FONTANA LAKE

IN THE SOUTHERN part of the Great Smoky Mountains National Park lies Fontana Lake, the southern border of the park, and also the boundary marker with the Nantahala National Forest. In addition to being an easy jumping off area for some of the wildest and most remote areas of the national park, the area along the lake contains some of the most unquestionably haunted areas in the park.

Of the dozens of former home sites and more than two hundred cemeteries(!) inside the Great Smoky Mountains National Park, the greatest concentration of each just happens to be located along the north shore of Fontana Lake. The eerie combo of the ruins of old home sites and small, seemingly forgotten cemeteries found deep in the woods is enough to creep out even experienced hikers and adventurers.

A rugged but fairly easy-going hike of a couple of miles along a well-established trail takes some courage—but if you really, REALLY think that you have what it takes, why not spend the night in a deep woods campsite right next to an ancient graveyard? Yes, you can do it—legally, even—in this part of the national park.

Start by taking the Norton Creek Trailhead, which begins at Lakeview Drive on the north shore of Fontana Lake. The six-mile hike upstream will lead you to both the Upper and Lower Norton Cemeteries. The trail itself is in good condition and is in actuality an old roadbed that's still in use around Memorial Day or other holidays when families of those buried in the deep, dark mountain graveyards come to pay their respects. In addition, this hiking route will also take you past many historical areas, complete with crumbling ruins, where sometimes only a partial wall or chimney remains. (Please be VERY careful around these old chimneys! They are fragile! Also, note that snakes, including the extremely poisonous timber rattler, seem to like hanging around old home sites.)

Once you arrive at the area, you can pitch a tent and make your campsite right inside the area some claim to be among the most haunted within the Great Smoky

Mountains National Park. There are several official backcountry camping sites, so be sure and inquire at the national park welcome center, or ask at any ranger station. Great Smokies park employees are among some of the friendliest in the entire nation, and will always go the extra mile to make sure you have the best and safest time possible in the park.

One of the more common modern ghost stories actually has a basis in the past. It's been said that, many years ago, one of the mountain settlers was accidentally killed in the woods while looking for his lost daughter in the area around what is now the north shore of Fontana Lake. To this day, it is reported that hikers who become lost along the trails on the north shore of the lake often encounter a "spook light," which miraculously guides them to safety. Those who have experienced the light believe it to be either the ghost of the settler or that of his daughter, tasked with forever wandering the woods to ensure that the same fate that befell the little girl doesn't happen again. My best advice would be to not get lost in the Smoky Mountains, but it does happen—if you're not fortunate enough to encounter a ghostly light to lead you to safety, try to remain in one spot—those who become lost in the woods tend to walk in circles, getting themselves even more lost and disoriented in the process. Try to never hike alone, and always, ALWAYS let someone know where you're going and when you expect to be back. Stay safe out there in the national park, kids!

The Fontana Lake area, along both shores, has too many stories to mention here regarding old home sites and cemeteries with creepy legends, Cherokee folktales, and local historical information. There are entire books written specifically about this extremely haunted area, which can be found via a simple online search of book vendors like Amazon or Barnes and Noble. Likewise, if you have ever had any strange encounters at Fontana Lake, please drop me a line!

CHAPTER NINE

HAUNTED ELKMONT RESORT

AT ONE TIME, the Elkmont Resort in the Great Smoky Mountains National Park was a big deal. It was a private social club and hunting association known as the Appalachian Club. The community and its wealthy and affluent "Gentleman Hunters" members could elect to stay at the lodge or obtain a parcel of beautiful mountain land on which to build their dream vacation home, with the club holding the lease on the property for at least ninety-nine years, with options to renew in perpetuity.

When both Tennessee and North Carolina began snapping up land in the 1920s and 1930s, prior to—but in anticipation of—the Great Smoky Mountains National Park, most of the mountain homes and farms of residents whose families had lived in the Smokies' various communities for several generations were purchased outright to be included in the national park. However, the land belonging to members of the Appalachian Club was under different negotiations, and club members could opt for a lesser payment that allowed them to keep the land for the lifetime of the current deed holder. Of the members of the club who took the "lifetime property lease" option, the last passed away in 1992, finally leaving the Elkmont community completely empty.

That being said, Elkmont might just be one of the creepiest and eeriest of the haunted areas to be found in the Great Smoky Mountains National Park. A spooky shadow of its once popular and thriving "resort within a resort" self, Elkmont now stands forlorn, sad and absolutely abandoned. The cabins, once belonging to the wealthy and affluent, now stand empty, doors ajar and windows missing, like some toothless apparition staring from the mountain mist, the stern US GOVT PROPERTY – NO TRESPASSING signs offering the only bit of color in this drab tableau.

Until about a decade or so ago, the remains and ruins of the once fantastical Wonderland Hotel stood, holding silent testament to the almost regal resort and vacation community that once stood in the area. Now, the Wonderland is all but completely vanished, having been demolished and bulldozed by the park service. The once grand hotel is now a blank square of earth that is slowly being reclaimed by the mountain laurel and trees and scrub brush.

The adventurous and daring souls that are searching for an active, very haunted spot will certainly want to put the remains of Elkmont near the top of their list when visiting the Great Smoky Mountains National Park. Try choosing a backcountry camping spot nearby and taking a walk through the wood around Elkmont in the middle of the night, where there have been reports of what sounds like a distant party, complete with casual conversation and the clink of ice cubes in tumblers. There are also spook lights, sometimes chasing away the curious, other times leading them farther afoot into the dark, dark woods, where it's all too easy to become lost and disoriented and to possibly disappear and to never be heard from again.

As always, stay out of areas marked NO TRES-PASSING—those signs are there for a reason—many of the old structures still standing are crumbling, and you could easily become trapped inside one of the cabins should a collapse occur. The wood floors are also very soft in places, making for other much-less-than-fun scenarios. Take note that the park service is very serious about these structures not being entered, and can have you arrested and fined for disobeying the posted signage.

As always with hiking in the mountains, try to never travel alone, and always, always let someone know where you're going and when you expect to return. Don't become another statistic or a new chapter in one of David Paulides *Missing 411* series (oddly enough, an interesting investigation into disappearances within public lands and many national parks, including the Great Smoky National Park).

CHAPTER TEN

HAUNTED LECONTE LODGE

MOUNT LECONTE IS a popular destination for a lot of hikers in the Great Smoky Mountains National Park, and with good reason—LeConte can only be accessed via hiking trails. One of the sole amenities at the top of a mountain in the beautiful wilderness of the Smokies, LeConte Lodge has provided many a hiker a place to lay their head for the night—but more than a few have reported a spectral visitor while spending the night in the shelter.

As the legend goes, if you're going to get a visit from the ghost of LeConte Lodge, she—the ghost of a little girl—will visit you at precisely 3:33 a.m. She doesn't say or do anything other than stare at you from the foot of your sleeping bag or pad or bedroll. Then, just as mysteriously as she appeared, she is gone.

Not much is known about the little girl ghost of Mount LeConte, other than she seems to have first begun appearing in the late 1960s or early 1970s. Many through-hikers of the Appalachian Trail have spotted the ghost of the sad little girl, and (from what I've heard) more than a few National Park Service employees have as well, although getting most of them to talk about the sightings may be a chore in itself.

There are several trails of varying degrees of difficulty that will take you to the top of Mount LeConte and to the lodge. For further information, I suggest checking out this wonderful website: http://www.lecontelodge.com

You may also inquire about trail conditions and difficulty at the Great Smoky Mountains National Park Welcome Center, or at any of the ranger stations located throughout the national park.

CHAPTER ELEVEN

HAUNTED CADES COVE

THE CADES COVE area of the Smokies is arguably one of the most beautiful and serene in all of the national park. Each fall, tourists come from all over the world to travel around the Loop, an eleven-mile one-way drive that encompasses Cades Cove and all the breathtaking autumn foliage the area has to offer. Apart from the idyllic, bucolic mountainside scenery—Cades Cove is also one of the most haunted areas within the national park borders.

Most likely, the area of Cades Cove is the most haunted on this list—what with abandoned cabins, ancient churches and overgrown graveyards making for a shocking contrast to the beauty of the mountains. While the local folks tell you that you don't want to be in Cades Cove after dark (or even at dusk, according to some), this is undoubtedly an area that the itinerant ghost hunter or intrepid legend tripper will want to include near the top of their "Must See and Do" list.

A brief search on the internet will reveal a shocking number of photographs from Cades Cove purporting to show paranormal activity. YouTube is loaded with videos offering the same. From orbs to apparitions to spook lights in the cemetery to buildings that aren't there to buildings that are there yet can't seem to be photographed at certain times—all await you in the eerie confines of the Cades Cove community.

Per the Great Smoky Mountains National Park section of the National Park Service website:

"Allow at least two to four hours to tour Cades Cove, longer if you walk some of the area's trails. Traffic is heavy during the tourist season in summer and fall and on weekends year-round. While driving the loop road, please be courteous to other visitors and use pullouts when stopping to enjoy the scenery or view wildlife.

"An inexpensive self-guiding tour booklet available at the entrance to the road provides a map and information about the cove.

"Only bicycle and foot traffic are allowed on the loop road until 10:00 a.m. every Saturday and Wednesday morning from early May until late September. Otherwise the road is open to motor vehicles from sunrise until sunset daily, weather permitting."

So, while it's only possible to remain in the area until sundown as of this writing (summer of 2020), there have been more than enough occurrences cited as happening in daytime hours to more than warrant a trip into the creepy cove. However, if you are feeling rather adventurous, camping is permitted nearby:

(Also from the National Park Service website, please verify for updates.)

Cades Cove Campground

• Open year round

• 159 sites

• Tents and RVs up to 35 feet

• Call (877) 444-6777 or visit http://www.recreation.gov to reserve a site.

Anthony Creek Horse Camp

• Call (877) 444-6777 or visit http://www.recreation.gov to reserve a site.

Backcountry Camping

• Reservation and permit required

• Call (865) 436-1297 for information

CHAPTER TWELVE

THE HITCHHIKING GHOST OF ROARING FORK MOTOR TRAIL

ROARING FORK MOTOR TRAIL is one of the lesser-known gems of the Great Smoky Mountains National Park. While very similar to Cades Cove in mountain beauty and wilderness grandeur, there are fewer crowds and less traffic along this scenic nature trail. Visitors rate this trail very high on the satisfaction scale and for its relaxing, scenic drive. While Townsend and Wears Valley take great pride in billing themselves "the quiet side of the Smokies," this area fits the criteria nicely as well. It's a beautiful mountain drive any time of year, but the views during the annual fall are exceptional indeed.

But I would be hesitant to include it in this volume if the Roaring Fork Motor Trail didn't have its own resident spook. While the Cades Cove and the Fontana

Lake areas probably have the most variety as far as active hauntings, the Roaring Fork Motor Trail has one of the creepiest stories in the Great Smokies area, possibly even spookier than Lydia, the sad little ghost at the Greenbrier Lodge (now known as the Greenbrier Restaurant, there's a chapter dedicated to it elsewhere in this book). Let's just say that if you were to see a lovely young girl asking for a ride back to Gatlinburg while on a Roaring Fork trip, be sure and find out if she's real before giving her a lift—otherwise, you may have just picked up the spirit of Lucy, the "phantom hitchhiker" of Roaring Fork Motor Trail.

The story is a familiar one and can be dated back even before the advent of the automobile—in the other versions of this story, the person asked for a ride may have been riding a horse or mule, or driving a wagon. In the end the results are still the same wherever the urban legend is repeated. A lone traveler, usually a male, sees a beautiful young girl on the side of the road and stops to give her a lift. After they part, the young man continues to think about the hitchhiking girl and becomes so obsessed that he returns to the area to find her. When he does manage to locate her house, he is met at the door by a parent, usually the mother, who informs the young man with sad news—yes, it was her daughter, but she passed away many years ago, on that very same road—and she's still trying to find her way back home.

Some variations include the young man being shown a photo of the girl, positively identifying her. In others, the young man also loans his coat to the young girl, only to be met with the same story from the mother the next day when he goes back to retrieve it. Under the mother's direction, he goes to the local graveyard and finds the girl's grave—and there, neatly folded on top of the grave and waiting for him—is the borrowed coat.

The local legend states that the young, beautiful Lucy perished in a cabin fire around the turn of the last century (some versions specifically state the year as 1909). To this day, it is said that Lucy still wanders up and down the Roaring Fork Motor Trail and has also been spotted off the trail a ways into the woods—this is supposedly the area where the cabin was located that burned, snuffing out her young life. It's also told that in the wintertime, the ghost will sometimes be seen walking along the trail barefoot—apparently perishing in a fire keeps even Lucy's spirit warm.

The trail is located just off Route 441. Enter from stoplight 8 at Historic Nature Trail Road (formerly Airport Road) in Gatlinburg / Great Smoky Mountains National Park, TN 70068.

Driving directions (from the Great Smoky Mountains National Park website): "From the main Gatlinburg Parkway (Hwy 441), make a turn at stoplight #8. You will follow Historic Nature Trail Road to the Cherokee Orchard entrance to the Great Smoky Mountains National Park. You will come upon signs to follow for the Roaring Fork Motor Nature Trail. The motor trail makes a loop and ends in Gatlinburg. At the stoplight, turn left onto Hwy 321 and you will return to the Gatlinburg Parkway."

More information can be obtained by calling (865) 436-1200 or by visiting the website at http://gsmnp. com/roaring-fork-motor-nature-trail.

CHAPTER THIRTEEN

TSALI, CHEROKEE GHOST

TSALI IS something of a legend in his native Cherokee culture. He was a staunch supporter of the rights of the indigenous Cherokee of the Western North Carolina side of the Great Smoky Mountains and was an ardent organizer of his people against the US government and their push to remove native Cherokee from their lands in the mountains and relocate them in Oklahoma—this horrific march in which thousands of Cherokee sadly perished is known as "the Trail of Tears," due to the incredible amount of death and human suffering that was encountered along the way.

Tsali was leading the fight against General Winfield Scott and the cavalry under his command in 1838. The general had ordered his men to begin rounding up the Cherokee and sending them packing to Oklahoma.

Forced with possibly losing the battle, Tsali and a band of his resistance fighters escaped into the mountains, where they continued to vex the general and his men. Eventually, General Scott sent word to the Cherokee that if Tsali surrendered, he would allow the other members of his band to go free. So Tsali realized that most if not all of his men would die if he continued to resist. He surrendered, only to have General Scott order him put to death by firing squad.

It's been said that for the last 150 years or so since the incident, the spirit of Tsali roams the Western North Carolina range of the Great Smoky Mountains, seeking revenge. It is said that his spirit most often appears as a glowing ball of light that both evades anyone who comes close, as well as chasing people (white people, in particular) away, or leading them off into the wilderness to become hopelessly lost in the mountain wilderness.

CHAPTER FOURTEEN

HAUNTINGS ON THE PARKWAY

THIS IS one of those rare, true instances of art imitating life imitating art—sort of, in a touristy, commercial sense. There is a haunted attraction on the Parkway (US 441, the main drag through town that leads into the Great Smoky Mountains National Park), called—oddly enough —Hauntings on the Parkway. It is kind of jarring to see something so spooky and creepy looking right in the middle of a major tourist and resort town, but there it is, amongst all the funnel cakes and fudge shops and martial arts weapons and air-brushed T-shirts and taffy machines and socks made-while-you-wait and knife shops and Christian bookstores...

The show is also known simply as "Hauntings," or even "Hauntings Extreme Ghost Show," and runs about every twenty minutes or so year-round, during normal business hours. The show itself is considered to be cheesy by many, but will usually scare the pants off any small children you might have with you, so there's that... What really makes the "attraction" shine is when you know some history behind this kind of spook show and realize that, for a short time during the early twentieth century, people actually believed in this sort of thing.

It's no different, really, than going to see a spirit medium perform a séance back in the time when the Spiritualism Movement was in its infancy. You are ushered into a room with carpeted benches with a bunch of other folks. The medium tells you that the séance is about to begin and cautions you against doing anything stupid, like taking a flash photograph during the show. The lights go down, creepy music is heard, and the festivities start. Glow-in-the-dark Ping-Pong balls sail through the darkened space, just above the heads of the audience. Musical instruments, including a tambourine and bugle, are seen to float in the air and play themselves. Disembodied voices come from all directions. A question an audience member wrote previously on a small slate chalkboard is answered aloud... and then the lights come up. Thank you all for coming, hurry back now, you hear?

All in all, the show lasts about ten minutes. I think it's worth the money, if only for the historical significance and the chance to laugh at how gullible our ancestors were when it comes to matters of the supernatural realm. These days, mediums are "channels," and the entity simply speaks to the waiting throng—no darkened room or floating musical instruments or ectoplasm necessary—the "show" element is gone—so maybe the real question is who is *most* gullible?

Now for the really spooky part. The Hauntings attraction opened on the Parkway in the late 1970s to robust business and is one of the longest running attractions in existence in Gatlinburg. Legend has it that in the early 1980s, one of the managers of Hauntings (I have heard the name "David" mentioned in reverent whispers) stayed late one night after the attraction closed to do some sort of thing that managers do after hours. Unfortunately for the manager, he just happened to suffer a fatal heart attack and died right there on the floor inside the attraction, behind one of the carpeted benches, near the wall in the back.

The legend continues that since this now-deceased manager was supposed to open the next day, there was a line of tourists waiting for the attraction to open, and the employees began to freak out because opening and the first show times had come and gone. Someone ran for a payphone up the street next to Fannie Farkle's Funnel Cakes, Mountain Corndogs and Video Arcade (no, really—it's a real place—or at least it was at one time) and called the assistant manager, who sped down the hill from East Gatlinburg (actually, to me, this is the least likely part of the legend—if you've ever been to Gatlinburg, traffic is usually such that one does not speed anywhere), and unlocked the doors. The employees rushed in, followed by the audience, and the show began. It wasn't until one of the employees, a "ghost" dressed head to toe in a "black suit" made of stretchy material, even covering the face, so as to remain invisible while flouncing about in the dark, banging a tambourine and tossing glow in the dark Ping-Pong balls, actually *tripped* over the deceased manager's body.

Realizing they had a real live dead person (ha-ha) in their midst, the employees and the audience panicked and fled on to the crowded Gatlinburg sidewalk. Although the tourists (and several of the employees) ran away never to return, the assistant manager (Brad, perhaps? That seems like a good name for an assistant manager), stayed behind until the authorities and ambulance and officials arrived to sort things out. It was shortly after all this commotion that other managers, the employees and even some of the audience members began to realize they were getting some extra bang for their Hauntings buck...

As one might gather, being left not only overnight in

the building, but actually becoming a part of the show the next day, made the newly deceased manager's spirit very angry. It's said that the Hauntings attraction really is, indeed, haunted. The real haunting events happen at random times and include cries for help and the smell of cigar smoke. People (audience members and performers alike) have reported being touched in the darkened theater space. The real hauntings should not be confused with the fake hauntings, which are part of the show. While you are not guaranteed to witness any phenomena from the actual haunting, you will enjoy things that your great-grandmother used to do when trying to contact her uncle Earl, who never returned to the farm after World War I.

Following the man's unfortunate death, employees began to observe real unexplained phenomena. Items put away the night before would be found tossed about upon opening. The next day, a disembodied voice was heard at times coming from the empty auditorium. After closing, female employees reported being touched lightly by a visible pair of hands when alone in the office, but perhaps the strangest incidents were the ones with the aforementioned spirits slides. After being wiped clean and put away after the performance, they would later be found with odd words written on them.

The word most often found was the name David,

the name of the dead night manager. As word of these occurrences spread amongst the locals, Hauntings found it hard to keep employees after changing hands. A couple of times with the same result, the business was unfortunately forced to close its doors forever.

Now (as of this writing) the building houses a laser tag establishment. It's a distinct possibility that the gamers are oblivious to the building's scary past and may have unknowingly experienced paranormal activity. Perhaps female players still feel invisible fingers gently caressing them in the dark. And maybe, just maybe, the disembodied voice of David's lonesome ghost still cries out.

The building is located at 716 Parkway, Reagan Terrace Mall, Gatlinburg, TN 37738. The phone number for the attraction is (865) 436-4636.

AS OF THIS WRITING, there are no less than three "haunted tours" operating in the Gatlinburg area. From my understanding, each one is fairly unique, although I do suspect there will be some overlap, even with all the scary things and hauntings that have happened in this sleepy little mountain resort town. I won't recommend any particular one over the others, as they all look to be a lot of fun as well as entertaining and educational. If you have the time and will be in Gatlinburg for three or more evenings, I recommend you try all of them out—it's a great way to spend a spooky evening in the mountains after a day of viewing the beautiful fall foliage the Smokies offer. In no particular order, here they are:

GHOST AND HAUNT Tours of Gatlinburg

Located at 404 Historic Nature Trail, Gatlinburg, TN

Phone Number: (865) 661-1980

Web: http://www.ghostandhaunt.com/

YouTube: https://youtu.be/iY-skp4XrMM

GHOST WALK of Gatlinburg

Meet at White Oak Cemetery, Gatlinburg, TN

Phone Number: (865) 556-0674

Web: http://www.ghostwalkofgatlinburg.com/

HAVE fun on all of these wonderful ghost walks, and please drop me a line and let me know what happened—I'd love to hear your story!

PART 2

MYSTERIES & LEGENDS

CHAPTER FIFTEEN

THE STRANGE LEGEND OF JUDACULLA ROCK

WAY UP in the mountains of Jackson County, near Sylva, North Carolina, there exists a giant, mysterious stone. What makes this large rock so mysterious is that it's literally covered with weird marks and pictures that scientists believe to be thousands of years old—perhaps tens of thousands. Even Cherokee Indians think that the area is ancient, as they claim the rock was already there when the tribe moved into the area long, long ago.

This large soapstone boulder, filled with an array of strange symbols and writing, has been called "... one of the greatest archaeological mysteries of the North American continent..."

Everyone from college professors to code breakers to mountain shamans have tried—and failed—to decipher the meaning and true origin of Judaculla Rock.

Is it written in code from ancient people, or perhaps ancient astronauts, as a message or warning to those of us here in the future? Maybe it's even Stone Age graffiti or even an advertisement: "See Rock City," indeed.

While no one can say for sure, the Cherokee have a legend that the carvings were done by a "slant-eyed giant with seven fingers on each hand" who once inhabited the area (contrary to popular belief, the giant most likely wasn't a resident of nearby Cosby or even a Walmart shopper). The legend continues that the giant, named Judaculla, was also the "Great Lord of the Hunt" and dominated the mountains back in those days. Judaculla was a powerful being and could jump from one mountain to the other, and could even create whatever weather phenomenon he desired. It's said that the giant even used the rock once to steady himself, leaving his seven-fingered handprint on the soapstone in the process. This is the same seven-fingered hand that Judaculla used (along with the talons on his feet, the legend says) to carve all the strange symbols and weird figures on the rock.

As it turns out, the Cherokee are not the only people to consider the site of the rock as a sacred area. It's rumored that in modern times, the rock is used in strange and bizarre "secret" initiations in the dark of night by a number of secret societies, fraternal organizations, and even some student-led groups from Western Carolina University, which is located not too far away.

The local folks can tell you that—possibly because of these occult-like rituals—the stone has become somewhat of a paranormal "vortex" or hot spot, complete with weird noises, ghostly apparitions, strange lights around and even above the boulder—ghosts, UFOs, general creepiness... What more could you want from an already historically significant site? And, if that's not enough, there's an ancient cemetery just a hundred yards or so away, which is also purported to be actively haunted... If you have any interest in historical archeology, ancient peoples, folklore, and the paranormal (or all the above), then make sure you visit Judaculla Rock on your trip to the nearby Great Smoky Mountains National Park.

Here are driving directions, courtesy of Judaculla-Rock.com:

"From US 74, take Exit 85 to Business Route 23 through Sylva. Stay on 23 1.3 miles to NC 107, then turn left onto 107. Drive 8 miles south on 107 and take a left onto Caney Fork Road, County Road 1737. Go 2.5 miles then turn left onto a gravel road and drive 0.45 mile. The rock is on the right, and parking is on the left."

Please note that although Jackson County owns the

property that Judaculla Rocks sits on and you can visit totally free of charge, there are no toilets or concessions or anything other than the rock itself and a boardwalk-style viewing area. Please do not play on the rock—soapstone is very soft by nature, and human contact can result in speeding up the erosion of this ancient site.

CHAPTER SIXTEEN

THE LOST CHEROKEE SILVER MINE OF GREENBRIER COVE

JUST DOWN FROM where Greenbrier Road and Ramsey Prong Road intersect in the Great Smoky Mountains National Park lies an area known as Greenbrier Cove. Inside the cove area is where the legend states that Perry Schultz, a resident of nearby Sevier County, allegedly rediscovered a lost Cherokee silver mine. There are many weird tales surrounding the area, including mysterious disappearances, strange lights seen flickering amongst the trees, and the sounds of ghostly voices off in the distance when one is quite sure they are alone. It was once claimed that the Cherokee said, "If the white man knew what we Cherokee know, he could shoe his horses with gold," such are the riches that are in the mine.

While Schultz supposedly worked silver out of the mine in the dark of night, it's said his wife would stand lookout with a shotgun, lest anyone discover the secret location. As is usual with this type of legend, anyone and everyone who knew the exact location of the "lost silver mine of the Cherokee" took the secret with them to the grave, although there are allegedly "secret markings" carved into trees in the area that point the way to the seeker of the mine.

As a boy, I remember hearing my father and an elderly friend of the family talking about the mine. My father's friend, who had to have been in his eighties, claimed that he knew where the entrance to the mine was, but he was afraid to go back due to the area supposedly being cursed. He described having to crawl down in a narrow opening, crawl up a steep shelf, and then crawl back down again into where the workable area of the mine opened up. He claimed that every time he tried to go in, something weird would happen at the location (such as a flashlight with brand-new batteries refusing to work) and then something bad happening later (on this particular occasion, shortly after he returned home from attempting to enter the mine, his wife grew violently ill and had to be hospitalized). Mind you, this was a tough old mountain man, who had been raised without such luxuries as indoor plumbing or even electricity in hard-core Appalachia that would make Tobacco Road look like a Sunday school picnic—I respect the man enough that if he was afraid to go traipsing about in the mine, then I'm afraid to go there too...

Should you still decide to visit the area and have a look around, the park rangers will point you in the right direction, but keep in mind that even if you *do* find the mine, you'd be hard-pressed to be able to mine it legally in the national park. Also bear in mind that the area is very rough going and is more or less encapsulated by knobby, rough, and twisted rhododendron groves, which the old-timers of the Smokies referred to as "hells"—and with appropriate reason, with one longtime park ranger having remarked, "I wouldn't send my worst enemy in there..." I suppose that even if you don't go to look for the lost silver mine, you can go to try to witness the paranormal that seems to be associated with this (and many other) lost treasures.

Keep in mind that the road conditions can be very rough at certain times of the year and can go from passable to impassable in a matter of minutes. The nearby Greenbrier Picnic Area provides a good staging area, as well as some accessible and easy trail hiking. Also take note that black bears as well as venomous timber rattlers and copperhead snakes are not uncommon in this area, so always check in at the nearest ranger station, keep an eye on the weather, don't hike alone, and always let someone know where you're going and when you expect to be back—there have been several unexplained disappearances in the Smokies—don't become the next one.

CHAPTER SEVENTEEN

THE LEGEND OF THE FIREFLY

EVERY SUMMER, visitors to the Great Smoky Mountains National Park are treated to a light show that is almost as amazing as the aurora borealis and almost as mysterious as the legendary Brown Mountain Lights in nearby western North Carolina. I'm writing of the synchronous fireflies (aka "lightning bugs") species indigenous to the Great Smokies and the only firefly species in America whose individual bugs can synchronize their flashing light pattern with nearby neighboring bugs, to the greater good of all the fireflies involved.

The synchronous fireflies (*Photinus carolinus*) are one of more than a dozen different types of fireflies that make their home in Great Smoky Mountains National Park. Curiously, this species is said to be the only species in North America whose individual insects can synchronize the patterns of their flashing lights, which amounts to quite an amazing show.

Fireflies (which we also refer to as "lightning bugs" in the South) are in fact a type of beetle. While they may take a year or two to mature from their larval stage, sadly they only live about three weeks after reaching full adulthood. During their journey as larvae, they feed on a smorgasbord of small insects, but no longer eat after making the transformation into adults, which may account for their short lifespan at that stage in their existence.

These strange synchronized lighting displays are made regarding their mating. Every individual species of firefly has a unique flashing pattern that helps the females and males to find each other from their own groups.

The majority of lightning bugs have a yellowish-green light, although there are some rarer species whose light appears a pale blue. As part of their mating ritual, the females remain in one spot while flashing, and the males flash as they fly around looking for a matching pattern.

Peak season for viewing these synchronous flashing fireflies in the Great Smoky Mountains National Park normally occurs during an approximate two-week period from late May to mid-June; however, it can happen earlier or later depending on factors such as weather and temperature.

The strange, almost eerie-appearing light the fireflies give off is a type of bioluminescence. While fireflies are the most commonly known creature that possesses this wild talent, there are other instances, such as glow-worms, fish, and snails. Even certain types of fungi and rotting wood can produce bioluminescence, which in the hills and hollers of the Smokies is referred to as "foxfire."

Although the fireflies in the Smokies do not always flash in unison, it's still an amazing sight to see as the flashes come in what appear to be wave patterns throughout the trees and hills. Sometimes after a very vivid flashing display, they all abruptly go dark for a short period of time. It's a must-see if you're in the Great Smokies during the right time of year, and is both strange and educational—fun for the entire family.

CHAPTER EIGHTEEN

THE LEGEND OF SPEARFINGER

"UWE LA NA TSIKU. *Su sa sai.*
  Liver, I eat it. Su sa sai.
  Uwe la na tsiku. Su sa sai."
  —Spearfinger

ASK MOST any Cherokee child living in the area of the Great Smoky Mountains, and he or she will be able to tell you the legend of Spearfinger. I'd guess that the majority of adult Cherokee can tell you the legend as well—Cherokee parents have been telling it in order to scare kids for more than the past one hundred years. I can remember asking my father, himself one-quarter Cherokee, why parents always tell their kids such frightening legends and stories. His answer was a simple one and probably the most correct—

"When you grew up poor in Appalachia, your parents had to tell you something to scare the daylights out of you to get you to lie down and shut up and go to sleep at night. A day's worked started well before daylight, and nothing would have gotten done if we kids had laughed and giggled and ran around all night like wild Indians."

Like I said, sounds like a good explanation to me. It made even more sense when I became a father—there's just some inherent fun about scaring your kids with tales about ghost and haunts like my parents did to me.

Spearfinger is the spirit of an old witch who is said to roam the Norton Creek Trail and Whiteside Mountain areas of the Great Smoky Mountains National Park. The legend of Spearfinger, especially when told during the dark of night while camping deep within the Smokies, may just be the scariest Cherokee folktale in existence.

Spearfinger is rumored to have a long sharp piece of obsidian rock as her right pointer finger, and it's been knapped into a long sharp knife blade, hence her name. It's said that the witch lurks in the shadows along the trails and deep woods of the Smoky Mountains, her teeth and mouth permanently stained a deep, scarlet red

—blood, from all the children she's managed to steal away from their parents—she uses her long, sharp knife of a finger to extract and then eat their livers. If that doesn't get a kid's attention right there, nothing will.

It is also told in the legend that Spearfinger always keeps her right hand clenched tightly, as her very heart is hidden beneath the skin of her palm, and she must protect it at all costs. Because of this part of the legend, it is said that the Cherokee are leery of anyone who may have strayed too long or too far from their own village, as Spearfinger is not only a witch who steals and eats children's livers, but also has the ability to skin walk or shape-shift, providing her the ability to assume the form of anything she wants, including your best friend or family member. If your parent or sibling or pal has been gone from the campsite for a long time, it might be a good idea to ask to see the palm of their right hand when they finally return to camp. If Spearfinger has, indeed, assumed the form of the person in question, she will flee before revealing her open palm.

Aside from shape-shifting into a family member, loved one, or friend, another favorite trick of Spearfinger is to disguise herself as a friendly grandmotherly lady who has lost her way along the trails. Her favorite tactic in this case is to try to also lure children away, under the guise of helping her back to her cabin, which she assures the child "is just a little ways away," and that their parents won't miss them on such a quick trip, there and back. Once you fall for the seemingly harmless old lady's ruse, it's hello Spearfinger, goodbye liver, and you're never seen or heard from again. It kind of puts a different spin on all those missing persons stories from the Great Smoky Mountains, doesn't it?

For trips into the very lair of Spearfinger, inquire about the current conditions of the Norton Creek Trail and Whiteside Mountain areas at the national park welcome center or at any ranger station. The wonderful park service employees will be more than happy to point you on the way should these areas be accessible during the time in which you wish to visit. Please be aware that, due to the weather and other factors, the conditions of trails and amenities within the Great Smoky Mountains National Park can literally change without warning. Make your trip a safe one and live to tell the tale!

CHAPTER NINETEEN

HUGGINS HELL

NOW HERE IS A REALLY strange one. Huggins Hell is a passage in the Great Smoky Mountains National Park that most guidebooks do not even mention. The rangers of the National Park Service may deny its very existence to you... And with good reason—unless you're a Navy SEAL or the most experienced of mountaineers (think those that have conquered Everest), they won't want you to try to attempt something as foolhardy, dangerous—and downright deadly—as attempting the climb through Huggins Hell. When the passage is mentioned, even by those few capable of traversing it, the famous phrase "Abandon all hope, ye who enter here" (from Dante's *Inferno*) springs to mind. Granted, there are a few people on the internet who have made the perilous climb (and even have amazing, death-defying pictures and selfies to prove it—pics or it didn't happen!), but it's definitely not your Sunday school picnic hike.

Much like many other places with so-called "devil names," Huggins Hell seems to garner the evil name from the harsh mountain area. You'll find that places with these "sinister" names tend to carry some sort of legend or story—sometimes to the point that it's difficult to determine if the evil name causes evil events or vice versa. Those in the Great Smoky Mountains National Park who choose to take this little-known trail to Mount LeConte face true risk of certain death or dismemberment. The climb itself takes even the most seasoned off-trail hiker a good four hours, the climb steep and perilous. Although a fall from the cliffs would almost assure immediate death, even if one were to survive, it's very possible that no one would find you or could even get to you if they knew where you landed during the fall —I can't imagine a worse fate than slowly dying at the bottom of a steep cliff face, unable to move because of internal injuries or a broken back and/or neck. A very chilling thought indeed.

The toughest part of the trail is inside the rushing stream that literally falls down the mountain. Due to the very nature of the water, even those who have survived the climb state that there is no right or wrong route through the rhododendron tangles, the stinging nettles, the yellow jackets and possibly snakes (timber rattlers and copperheads are common in the Great Smokies)—simply a series of choices that one must make correctly, that not only change from climb to climb, but can change from minute to minute due to the rushing stream.

As to the hauntings, no one is sure when they initially began, or who the spirits sometimes spotted in the area might have belonged to in a previous life—the best educated guesses are that the ghosts are of those who tried—and sadly, failed—to negotiate the area known as Huggins Hell. Due to the sheer danger and very likely risk of severe injury up to and including death, I have chosen not to give away the exact spot where Huggins Hell is located. It can be found if one is persistent (and perhaps foolhardy) enough, but if you choose to go ghost hunting in the area, I would strongly recommend sticking to the ground in lower elevations. Stay safe, boys and girls, stay safe.

CHAPTER TWENTY

CHEROKEE LEGEND OF THE "LITTLE PEOPLE"

A COMMON TALE among all the indigenous native people, seemingly throughout the world—stories of "little people" abound. The Irish have their leprechauns, the Nordic folk have their gnomes and elves, and many other societies and cultures share similar folk legends and tales. The Cherokee, in particular, have a huge wealth of myths and legends, some of which go back not just centuries, but thousands and tens and hundreds of thousands of years even, to when the planet was formed and how all the different systems of nature on our planet Earth work.

The ancient Cherokee, whom—as far as is known—are the first people to inhabit the Great Smoky Mountains National Park, have a legend or a story for everything you can imagine: animals, insects, plants, trees, flowers, herbs, mountains, creeks, lakes, rivers, etc., etc. ad infinitum. The rich oral tradition of the Cherokee people have insured that these tales are passed down from generation to generation. Even in the twenty-first century of high technology, there are initiatives underway to make sure that all the Cherokee legends and stories are recorded for posterity.

One of the most fascinating—and eerie—stories in the Cherokee legend repository are the various and numerous accounts of what the Cherokee call the "Yunwi Tsunsdi," which roughly translates into English as the "Little People." In the stories of old (and even into modern day), these entities are sometimes described as being from the ethereal plane, but other times the Cherokee consider them to be a small, humanlike race of people, about two to four feet high. Some versions of the Cherokee even have the little people initially arriving in the area aboard a "flying, silver disc," so perhaps the little folk of the Smokies are actually little men from Mars?

These "little people" of legend are also believed to be shape-shifters of a sort, and use this to their advantage when deciding what form to assume. According to the Cherokee legends, each of these little people can morph into three or four different types of spirits or entities. While sometimes the little people can be helpful (it seems they are especially good at finding lost articles if plied with certain foods or drinks as a reward), seeming to give preference to small children and the very old and/or infirm, these selfsame little folk can turn mean and dangerous at the drop of a hat if they are disrespected or feel like their space has been intruded upon. Oddly enough, like the little men Rip Van Winkle came across playing tenpins in the forest, the little people of the Great Smoky Mountains are said to possess the very power to cloud the human mind, resulting in confusion. There are even those among the Cherokee tribe who believe this is why people are at risk of going missing in the Great Smoky Mountains National Park—you have upset the little people and will be allowed to wander the wilderness for your transgressions against them. A rather chilling thought, isn't it?

Said to have the aforementioned ability to disguise themselves in a number of ways, the little people have the ability to remain invisible and undetected in general (unless surprised by the sudden appearance of a human, for example). There are times, however, that they can and do choose to reveal themselves to the populace at large—when this happens, there is usually not a single sighting, but a sudden flap or wave of sightings over a short period of time, which then subsides. Some claim that these "mass sightings" only occur every generation or so, then the little people, satisfied that they have scared and confused the humans, go back into hiding and enjoy their peaceful mountain ways.

It is also said in the legends and stories that the little people live as close to nature as possible, which would explain their fondness for such beautiful wilderness amongst the mountaintops and streams of the Great Smoky Mountains. They seem to be very spiritual beings by nature, and even when they do attempt to teach humans a lesson, the lesson will contain certain aspects of traits they feel we need as a people: respect, kindness and, above all, a joy for life and living. When the little people are spotted by humans, it usually seems to be because they are so enraptured with the activity they are involved in at the time—some common examples of sightings of the little people have them involved in dancing, singing, or some form of drumming or otherwise making "nature music."

They live close to nature, in the forests and mountains. They have a spiritual aspect to them, and they try to teach humans about kindness, joy and respect. The little people like to dance to rhythmic drumming and music.

While there is no one particular place that is any better than any other to spot the little people in the Great Smoky Mountains, areas with the most untamed nature seem like the best bet—Cades Cove, the North

Shore of Fontana Lake, the deep woods near Elkmont, LeConte and Clingmans Dome... Interestingly enough, these areas are also purported to be among the most haunted within the national park. Perhaps the spirits of the natural and the spirits of the supernatural both walk hand in hand among the dark forests and quiet glens of the Great Smoky Mountains National Park. If you do happen to be one of the few who are fortunate enough to spot the little folk, remember to keep your distance and do not approach them, lest you be mesmerized and left to wander about the mountains, perhaps forever. Reverence and respect should keep you safe. While this may sound tongue-in-cheek to our modern ways and means, the Cherokee did (and still do) take the cautionary tales very seriously, sometimes avoiding certain places in the mountains altogether. Stay safe out there!

For additional information regarding these stories and legends, I highly recommend the 1998 book *Cherokee Little People: The Secrets and Mysteries of the Yunwi Tsunsdi*, written by Lynn King Lossiah and Ernie Lossiah. The authors take a serious, scholarly (yet wholly enjoyable) look into the phenomena as they share a veritable bonanza of all the wonderful Cherokee myths and legends in which the little people are known to have played a central part.

CHAPTER TWENTY-ONE

OF WILD MEN AND FERAL CANNIBALS

FOR DECADES, tales of mysterious people inhabiting the deep woods of the Great Smoky Mountains National Park have persisted. These range all the way from reports of "hairy wild men" to entire families or groups of feral cannibals.

For some "conspiracy theorists," these wild, feral people are said to account for the unexplained disappearances in the national park. In particular they have been blamed for the disappearance of young Dennis Martin, the six-year-old boy who vanished near the Cades Cove area in June of 1969 (this case is discussed in greater detail elsewhere in this volume). A cryptic YouTube channel named South Force 10 elaborates on this theory and even claims to have inside knowledge.

Even retired park ranger and legendary tracker

Dwight McCarter (who was the lead in the Dennis Martin disappearance and many others during his long career) admits that there were "wild men" who lived deep within the recesses of the national park.

Some claim that these "wild men" are in fact the cryptic creature also known as Bigfoot. There have been Bigfoot sightings throughout the whole of Appalachia, so if the creature does indeed exist, the Great Smokies National Park would be the perfect area for it (or them) to inhabit.

The Cherokee have legends and stories of these "hairy giants" who were already inhabitants of the land before the Cherokee came into the area thousands of years ago.

Other people claim that these "wild men" (some say there are women and children, too) are not Bigfoot at all, but rather inbred and untamed humans who have lived their entire lives deep in the woods. They dress in animal skins, hunt and forage for their food, build their own shelters and so on. Naturally, they don't take kindly to strangers and have been known to kill any interlopers who dare to enter their secret domain, whether by accident or design.

And they have been known to eat them as well.

Yes, that's correct. The rumors and legends and tales from the dark hills and hollers of the Great Smoky

Mountains (as well as other parts of Appalachia) are not only isolated, inbred, and demented—they lean toward cannibalism as well.

Although the average person will tell you that this is preposterous and there's no way humans (even wild, hairy, inbred ones who have the occasional craving for human flesh) could hide out in the mountains undetected. I counter with this: have you ever been to the Smokies?

Now, I'm not talking about Gatlinburg or any of the touristy areas. I'm not even talking about the myriad of trails that run through the park, which are hiked by millions of hikers every year. I'm talking about deep in the woods, really deep. There are places off-trail that it's possible no human has ever set foot—not even the settlers or Cherokee or possibly even bigfoot, if he exists.

The Great Smoky Mountains National Park covers over half a million acres. Let that number settle in. Half a million. 522,427 acres to be exact, as per the National Park Service website. Unless you've been in the deep woods, where there are no trails, no markers, no anything other than you and the forest—it's almost impossible to comprehend just how vast this wilderness is indeed.

The ruggedness of the national park, which sits on the border of Eastern Tennessee and Western North

Carolina (in fact, it's almost divided evenly between the two states) has to be seen—nay, experienced—to be believed. It's in these giant old-growth forests that you begin to realize just how small and infinitesimal a person is compared to the wilderness. It's no wonder people die out here. Especially those who are ill equipped and ill prepared.

I said all that to say this—there are plenty of places—an almost innumerable number of places—that a person or even a group of persons could hide out for an indefinite amount of time. If you had the basic rough necessities—food, water, shelter (which are in abundance here if you know what you're doing)—there would be no reason to ever leave those woods.

Case in point:

Eric Robert Rudolph, also known as the Olympic Park Bomber, successfully hid out in the Nantahala National forest, which is a 533,000 expanse of wilderness in Western North Carolina, and along the Appalachian Trail heading toward the Great Smokies.

Rudolph managed to elude the FBI for five years and was only caught in 2003 because he left the forest and was rummaging through a trash dumpster in Murphy, North Carolina, where he was spotted by a rookie police officer who recognized him from the FBI 10 Most Wanted list.

If this man with only minimal survival skills managed five years, imagine the skills of someone who has never left these woods in their entire lives. As a possibility, it must be considered. Cases like this, hearing rumors even of the wild men and cannibals, families of people living like this their whole lives, makes me question our very humanity as a species. Did society and what the majority considers socially normal and or acceptable tame us and take away our very instincts and our human nature? At their base, feral humans are simply people who have grown up and lived their entire lives without any human contact aside from other ferals. Would things they participate in, like cannibalism, be so disgusting and unmentionable to us if it weren't ingrained into our head basically from the moment we are born that it's just those very things that are wrong and taboo and, well, gross? Let's take a closer look at these alleged sightings of these wild and feral people and communities, which seem to be springing up more and more in recent years, or at the very least taking the blame for what's going on with these missing clusters.

Though our focus is the Great Smokies, these communities and lone people are all over the world, in all of the deepest forests and woods. Sometimes they are even raised by animals, mainly wolves, and are therefore without any kind of human instincts to speak of. No morals, the morals of a wild beast, a feral animal who will attack at the scent of a human and or their blood, and this is most likely why these people are being blamed for many of the missing clusters.

One of the earliest reported accounts of a feral human is the somewhat obscure tale of a bizarre individual (do we even call them "human" at this point?) who came to be known as "Wild Peter." In 1724 in Germany, some men were hunting deep in the woods, what they were hunting for has been lost to time and retelling, but what they came upon that day has never been forgotten.

Imagine how startled and surprised these men were when out of some deep and thick woods emerged a small boy. He was on all fours like an animal and at first was only recognized by the men as "a naked, brownish black-haired creature." The men were astonished and tried their best to coax the wild boy out of the thicket so they could capture him. Their reasoning for wanting to do this is unknown. I wonder if they were going to help or harm him. I wonder if they'd have been safe had they been successful. It doesn't matter either way because the boy would not be caught that day; he was smart and wily enough to know danger. He sensed it, like a shark sensing blood across the entire ocean. The lad turned and ran at an inhuman speed back into the depths of the forest.

While the focus of this book is the Great Smoky Mountains, I think it's smart to know at least some history, so we can maybe come to some kind of acceptance that these things, these wild "people" DO exist, all around the world. In all of the places where there are people disappearing without a trace, in fact.

The boy was estimated to be about twelve years old, and when the men reported what they had seen, they found they weren't the only ones to have seen this boy creature. He had been a haunt to the area for a long time and was known to even climb trees with the ease of a bear, though he snarled and growled and walked on all fours like a wolf. The child was eventually captured by another group of hunters and brought to King George I himself, who was already visiting the area. The king was fascinated by the child, who was particularly fond of eating raw vegetables and meat, who had no concept or knowledge of speech, and who seemed to love to tear apart and devour live birds.

King George loved the little creature boy and named him Peter. He was shipped off to England to be studied by the best and most well-respected academics. The thing about "Peter," though, was that he was also a pickpocket. How did he learn this behavior? He wouldn't eat bread or anything cooked and abhorred being bathed.

What is my point of telling the tale of Wild Peter? Just to show that this has been going on most likely since the dawn of time. I think with technology it's just becoming harder to hide. It's becoming harder for these lone people or their communities to stay off the radar. Anyways, back to the Smokies.

On July 13, 1973, a seasonal national park ranger named Charles Hughes had a violent encounter with "the Wildman of Cataloochee." While checking up on fishermen, looking for licenses, he encountered a large man with a heavy beard and a fly rod. Hughes asked for the man's name and whether or not he had a fishing license. The man replied, "I've got no name. I've lived in these woods all my life." When asked about the fishing license, the man reached into his jacket and pulled out a pistol. Though the ranger managed to disarm the man during a scuffle, he wasn't able to fully subdue him. As Hughes tried to drive off in his Jeep to get assistance in detaining the "man," a giant rock was thrown through the Jeep's window.

Hughes was able to get to a nearby station for backup, and a large group of rangers and volunteers used bloodhounds and tracked the wild man well into the night. They were never able to find any trace of him.

Subsequently a popular song came out of the encounter, and of course much discussion and speculation about the encounter came out in public through the press. This story and many more live on and have been added to and exaggerated upon to this very day. Despite these additions to the story, the fact remains the same, these men and children and even women do exist, and they are seemingly very dangerous to encounter.

There is another side to all of this as well; thus far we have been talking about the feral and wild people who have lived their entire lives in the wilderness and have no idea of civilization, some of whom were even taken in and raised by wild and deadly animals. This seems to defy Mother Nature herself, but what about the people who choose to "live off grid" and purposely set out to live wild and possibly feral? There are so many reports, especially in recent years, of encounters with these wild and or feral men. Does the ease with which they are able to accomplish this and their ability to just slip into this life of no contact with humanity and no creature comforts or worldly pleasures just show us that we are one step—maybe even one accidental slip—from being this way in the first place? Is wild and feral living what humanity was really made for?

The concept of people choosing to live this way is something most of us can't even fathom, yet it fascinates us nonetheless. Fascinates and terrifies us. Jeff Holland has a rather famous account of his encounter with a "feral human" in the heart of the Appalachian mountains, which he describes in detail in his book *Weird Kentucky*. It happened right near Cloudsplitter Rock in 1990. The author says he encountered a white male in his mid to late thirties naked but for being covered in leaves, mud and vines. These were also matted into his hair and beard, both of which were filthy and unkempt, as much of the young man's appearance was. Holland described the man as having an "absurd 'Swamp Thing' appearance." The wild man's walk was apelike and hunched over. After maintaining eye contact for "what seemed like an eternity," the apelike feral man turned and ran off into the depths of the woods and forests.

This brought up an interesting thought for me. Is this how they're able to kidnap and stalk humans so easily? Thinking about the description both Jeff Holland and many others have given of these "people," it came to my attention how easily they would just blend into the environment. I have a strong and strange feeling that somehow if they do not want to be seen, they won't be. Of course, one can be caught by surprise every now and again, but the reports are almost always the same, with a few exceptions here and there, that they turn and run, at an almost inhuman and catlike speed, back into the wilderness from which they came. It brings me back to Dennis Martin and the "wild man" the Key family had described in their witness report. A park ranger had been attacked by such a man just a year earlier in the exact same spot from where Mr. Key had observed this thing with "something" on its back.

We must also keep in mind what the Great Smokies were BEFORE they became a national park. It was actually a mountain range that was full of mountain communities, which were thriving, such as Cades Cove and Cataloochee. If you go all the way back to the 1700s, you'll find a very different atmosphere than today, and that's putting it lightly. Hernando De Soto discovered the Cherokee tribes in the Smokies during his 1540 exploration, which brought the European settlers into the area. Those of the Cherokee who didn't want to adapt and conform to European culture of the time were forced to go to Oklahoma, which is what the trail of tears is. Fast-forward to the early 1900s and you'll see the people finally start to utilize the beautiful and bountiful resources of the land. They were farming, hunting, raising livestock, and even cutting down the trees to build their own homes. Forests then became towns and pastures, none of which you will see there today. As the years went by, farming gave way to lumbering.

As logging towns began popping up all over the

Smokies, inevitably the geography started to transform, and much of the forests had been cleared away, with nothing replanted to grow in their place. At the rate they were clearing and logging, the trees would have become extinct and there would be no national forest like we know today, at least not the Great Smokies. In 1934 Congress and Franklin Roosevelt chartered and dedicated the park to protect it from being cleared and built on anymore. Is it so much of a stretch to believe that some people are more interested in living as our ancestors did in the Smokies back in the 1500s, 1600s, 1700s and so on?

CHAPTER TWENTY-TWO

LEGENDS OF THE CHEROKEE

THE CHEROKEE TRIBES, *who live in the Western North Carolina side of the Great Smoky Mountains, have an amazing number of myths and legends that have been passed down over the centuries. There are so many, it would be impossible to list them all due to the size constraints of this volume. However, I've decided to include some of the more strange and esoteric legends here:*

—UKTENA

One of the more interesting legends of the Cherokee is that of the Uktena, an animal that looks like a cross between a snake and a dragon with horns. There are a multitude of legends about these beasts, but the origin states that Uktena was originally a man who was changed due to his trying—and failing—to destroy the sun. In Cherokee folklore tradition, there are many tales of Cherokee braves killing one of these horned-dragon serpents. The monsters are very evil and seek nothing more than to track and destroy human prey for sport. Not limited to one area of the mountains, the Uktena can show up and attack most anywhere and at any time.

—ANIYVDAQUALOSGI

A type of spirit thought to be similar in action to the "thunderbirds" of the Southwest, but are different in appearance. The name translates to "Thunderers," and these flying spirits can bring down thunder and lightning on the hapless inhabitants of the mountains below. Sometimes, these entities can take human form and walk the mountains among the Cherokee. While considered dangerous to other types of flying beasts and giant terrors, the Aniyvdaqualosgi are believed to be friendly toward people unless provoked.

—TLANUWA

These giant birds of Cherokee myth and legend are similar to the "firebirds" and "thunderbirds" described by native American tribes of the Southwest portion of the country. It has also been noted that, due to the problems the Cherokee had in defending against these birds due to their "impenetrable skin," they may be a type of flying dinosaur, such as a pterodactyl. There are claims of these flying giant birds having been spotted in the higher elevations of the Great Smoky Mountains, often sailing from peak to peak. The birds are hunters and will take humans as prey, and have been known to vex entire villages until driven away by Cherokee braves.

—YUNWI TSUNSDI

While the name literally translates to "the little people," the story of the Yunwi Tsunsdi is very well known and often told among the native Cherokee in the Great Smoky Mountains area. Very similar to what are known as elves, fairies, dwarves and gnomes in other cultures, these are earth spirits that can (and very often do) take the form of small humans. Although they usually prefer to remain hidden (and have the power to become invisible at will), they will sometimes choose to reveal themselves to the lost or weary traveler or hiker in the Great Smoky Mountains. According to the stories, the only time that the small humans choose not to be helpful is if they are threatened or feel disrespected in some way. Although not evil, if angered, they have been known to lure both children and adults off the trail, never to be seen again. I have dedicated a whole chapter to the Yunwi Tsunsdi elsewhere in this book, titled "Cherokee Legend of the Little People."

CHAPTER TWENTY-THREE

THE GREAT SMOKIES TRIANGLE?

ARE *the Great Smoky Mountains cursed? In addition to all the hauntings, natural disasters, murders, and disappearances that have happened within these dark hills and hollers, here are some more strange things to consider...*

WEIRD WEATHER like The Great Blizzard of 1993 – 24 Go Missing in the Great Smoky Mountains

It has many names, "the No-Name Storm," "the '93 Superstorm," "the Great Blizzard of 1993," and even "the Storm of the Century." Whatever you want to call it, the cyclonic storm that formed over the Gulf of Mexico in March of 1993 caused massive amounts of destruction and chaos. The storm was unique in so many ways. It was massive in size, extremely high in intensity, but most of all, how far and wide it reached was unheard of, and still is even to this day.

The storm formed on March 12, 1993, and didn't dissipate until three days later. During its strongest hour, it reached all the way from Canada to Honduras! It traveled through the eastern United States and then headed to eastern Canada. The heavy snow started as far south as Alabama and even northern Georgia. Birmingham, Alabama, reported thirteen inches of snow, it's incredibly rare for snow to fall at all in that area, and parts of Georgia reported having had a massive thirty-five inches fall to the ground. Even the Florida Panhandle reported up to four inches.

This storm was definitely unique... unique and deadly. With hurricane-force wind gusts and record low barometric pressure combined in some areas with scattered tornadoes, the storm was like the angel of death, and it claimed hundreds of lives. The largest recorded amounts of snowfall were located at Mount LeConte in Tennessee. A record fifty-six inches was reported to have fallen. At the tallest mountain in North America, Mount Mitchell in North Carolina, fourteen-foot snowdrifts accumulated, and fifty inches of snow were reported to have fallen.

The day after the deadly storm dissipated into the

North Atlantic Ocean, on March 16, 1993, rescuers restarted their air searches for twenty-one high school students and three faculty members who were trapped in the freezing cold and snow-drenched mountains. On the day before, military helicopters, having already made 120 trips in their rescue effort, had to cease their search. They weren't able to land anywhere near let alone on the dark and treacherous mountains. They had only been able to rescue ninety-three individuals, four of which were in the hospital and one of them, a teacher, was even in intensive care. The group was there on a trip from the Cranbrook Kingswood High School in Bloomfield Hills, Michigan.

Unfortunately because of the darkness and the inability for their rescuers to continue, the unfortunate remaining members of the party were facing yet another night trapped on this deadly alp we know as the Great Smokies. All they had to their names to provide shelter and cover were their individual ski jackets, sleeping bags, and tarpaulins that they had brought with them, which ironically they had brought with them for that very purpose. They had no idea how badly they'd need them, and more.

Back at home the parents tried to remain hopeful and upbeat, while holding all-night vigils at the Cranbrook Kingswood school. The hope was that those who still remained were hiking at lower altitudes than the ones who had already been rescued. Some had even emerged safely and unharmed all on their own. This would be the remaining hikers' fourth night stuck and trapped in the massive snow, with the temperatures expected to drop into the mid-forties. The chance for rain and/or snow increased as the night wore on.

Luckily, all of the hikers had been trained in wilderness survival and first aid. They were also fairly equipped for extreme weather. Phone lines were down, and trees were all over the roads, blocking the trailheads in the park. This made the news of who had been rescued and who still remained trapped not only in short supply, but when it did come, it was often contradictory.

Eventually all 124 people were rescued and survived with little to no permanent damage. The Great Smoky Mountains are the most popular national park in the United States and just about eleven million visitors show up each year. It's a complete contradiction. Beautiful yet deadly. For a mountain range that gets its name because of the mists and fogs that provide it with a constant cover, it's important to remember to respect it in its entirety. After all, that very fog is one of the many dangers just lurking about in the mountains, waiting to claim lives. Luckily the end result of the trapped students and faculty of the Great Blizzard of '93 was a happy one, oftentimes people aren't so lucky.

———————

HOW DOES a beautiful and serene area designated for fun adventures like hiking and camping turn suddenly into an environment that threatens your very life, like what happened to the high schoolers in 1993? So many people are so concerned with worrying about the dangerous and admittedly oftentimes deadly wildlife, they forget what the two main causes of death in the great Smokies actually are. Automobile accidents and plane crashes. These are closely followed by things like lightning strikes, suicides, and even heart attacks. There is actually not one single report of a snake bite fatality in the history of the park and only one reported bear attack fatality.

These are some of the main things that hikers and campers set out prepared for, and the actuality of being bitten by a snake or attacked by a bear are less than slim and almost none.

What has been reported a whopping fourteen times, which is enough to cause anyone's spine to tingle... murders. It's not just the weather that can cause a relaxing day trip to turn into a life-threatening situation.

The National Park Service will be turning a whopping 105 years old this coming August, and with its birthday, it brings questions to mind. Questions I'm sure many of us have, mainly the loved ones of all of the people who have seemingly vanished into thin air from the parks. Perhaps the park rangers and even local law enforcement officials will be wondering about all of the unidentified and unclaimed bones and bodies that have been found throughout the more than a century of people flocking to the area of the Great Smokies specifically to have fun and party and possibly even go for a nice relaxing nature hike, only to end up never being seen again.

Take, for example, the first ever reported disappearance, which took place in the Great Smokies way back in June of 1969. In Spence Field, located in the park itself, Dennis Martin and his brothers were getting up to no good, as only small boys could do, planning on hiding long enough to be able to sneak up on and scare the wits out of their frantic family members, who would surely be looking for them while they tried to stifle their giggles and hide behind some trees nearby. When it was time for the boys to run out and startle the grown-ups, Dennis was nowhere to be seen. Despite the search effort covering an approximate fifty-six-mile area and including nearly 1,400 searchers, Dennis would never be seen again. Heavy rains on the first day and blinding mist on the second made the search efforts almost futile. Even with the National guard and Special Forces conducting their own searches, the boy seemed to have disappeared into thin air. Even today, fifty-three years later, it still remains the largest search effort in the history of the Great Smoky Mountains National Park.

On September 25, 1981, a fifty-eight-year-old woman named Thelma Pauline Melton was on a relaxing day hike with some friends near the Deep Creek Campground. All Pauline did was walk just a couple of steps ahead of her group of friends and continue on over a small hill. When the friends also made it over the hill, literally seconds later, Thelma had vanished. Often called "Polly," Thelma had known this land almost intimately. She had been hiking this exact same trail for over twenty years! So where did she go in just a matter of thirty to forty-five seconds? She had just moments ago been teased by her friends about her too slow pace, and suddenly she seemingly walked right out of existence in a matter of seconds. But there lies the mystery of the Smokies!

Whatever is taking these people is indiscriminate. Whatever is causing these strange and bizarre and seemingly random weather patterns doesn't seem to care about the pain and suffering of the loved ones left behind, with no answers and only memories to keep them comforted at night.

While many people use national parks for vacation spots to escape the stress and strain of everyday life, it's not uncommon for these seemingly simple camping or hiking trips to go horribly wrong in an instant, as we've just seen with Dennis Martin and Thelma Melton. They both seemingly disappeared into thin air, completely vanished without a trace. While we don't know what happened to those two, and many, many others who have met the same unfortunate demise, we know all too well what can happen when the weather turns for the worse just as quickly as these people seem to vanish.

In 2012 near the popular Cades Cove area of the park, a sudden and extremely violent thunder and lightning storm struck. Lightning took down so many trees it left many people trapped and injured. Two people even lost their lives. One moment it was sunny and beautiful, and these tourists were taking in the majestic scenery, letting the peacefulness in the air take them over, and within seconds a flash storm started. Ralph Frazier of Buford, Georgia, was riding his motorcycle when a falling tree limb struck him in the head and killed him on impact. Rachel Burkhart of Corryton, Tennessee, was swimming in a swimming hole when yet another tree limb was struck and fell on top of her, also killing her instantly. The same tree struck a seven-year-old little girl and knocked her unconscious; luckily her mother was able to revive her. The girl's father, however, wasn't as lucky, suffering from fractured vertebrae, multiple broken ribs, and a collapsed lung. The storm seemed to stop just as quickly and suddenly as it had started, yet many people were still trapped for up to five hours because emergency rescuers were unable to clear all of the fallen limbs and trees fast enough to get to them.

As I hope we have learned from this, it's not only human error and Mother Nature we have to worry about in the woods of any national park, especially the Great Smokies, which is the most visited. It's the unknown, that which we cannot prepare for because we cannot know or see it, that we should most fear. Be careful out there in the woods, even in broad daylight, watch your step, and NEVER separate from the group!!

CHAPTER TWENTY-FOUR

STRANGE PLANE CRASHES

MORE THAN FIFTY Planes Crashed in the Great Smokies

The Great Smoky Mountains are a mountain range rising along the Tennessee-North Carolina border located in the southeastern United States. They form a part of the Blue Ridge Physiographic Province and are a sub-range of the Appalachian Mountains. The Smokies are most known for being a part of the Great Smoky Mountains National Park, which is the most visited national Park in the United States with approximately eleven million visitors each year.

The park was established in 1934. Despite the majestic scenes and quiet and peaceful hiking trails and camping spots, there are quite a few dark sides to the Great Smokies. Ever hear of the Bermuda Triangle or the Bennington Triangle? You probably have; however, there is also talk of a possible Great Smokies triangle, evidenced by at least fifty or more plane crashes taking place in and around the mountain range as far back as records are kept. As we go through just a handful of the plane crashes, both deadly and otherwise, over the last fifty years, keep in mind the odds of getting in a plane crash are literally one in a million. Is there something sinister working against not just pilots but the rescue workers and rangers who attempt to save the injured or recover the deceased, lurking in the Great Smokies? Is it something supernatural, roaming around and waiting to feed off of the death and devastation that these crashes cause, in both the people directly involved and also the public?

IN 1946 A MILITARY plane crashed near Clingmans Dome in the national park. Though the wreckage has obviously been cleared away since then, you can still hike past it to this day. The B-29 Superfortress was a bomber plane built for the United States Army. It had four engines with a combined 8,800 horsepower and could fly at 220 miles per hour. This bomber had an extremely impressive 141-foot wingspan and was 27 feet high and 99 feet long. When the crash happened, the Superfortress was on a routine navigational night training mission, and everything should have been business as usual. However, while returning from MacDill to Chicago, the plane crashed in the early morning hours of June 12. At 2:16 a.m. it made its last radio contact, and that was with the Knoxville Airport. At this time, the mountains were cloud covered, and the forecast was calling for scattered thunderstorms. The plane suddenly began to hit treetops about one-eighth of a mile from the Clingmans Dome Observation Tower. When it hit the ground, it actually lost both of its wings and continued traveling a quarter of a mile and went right across the North Carolina border. Unfortunately, the fuselage's fuel tank ignited, which caused not only the plane but the surrounding forest to erupt into flames. This giant and spectacular Army bomber plane was shredded into at least a thousand pieces. All but one of its four engines were also mangled, with the surviving one having landed on the opposite side of the road. A park ranger recalled that the wreckage stretched across more than an acre of land, with all twelve people on board perishing.

SINCE THE INVENTION of the airplane, there have been more than fifty-four crashes inside the Great Smoky Mountains alone! There are also twenty more crashes that took place right outside the park itself. If you look all over the southern part of the Appalachians, you'll find scattered pieces of airplanes and bits of debris everywhere. There are also, still to this day, five or six crash sites and wreckages that have yet to be found! The main cause of crashes in this area is private pilots who are coming from flatlands into the misty mountains. The reason? Spatial disorientation. Because of the onset of the sudden mist, the pilots get lost in the clouds and seem to be directionless, not knowing which way is up or down. Is it really possible for such a magnificent piece of machinery to be literally shredded? Twenty crashes taking place right outside the park? Why this particular area of the Smokies? Surely for how large it is, if pilots really are more susceptible to crashes, be it due to weather or cloud cover or simple human error, wouldn't it be more probable that these events wouldn't be so localized? After all, you're more likely to be killed by a meteorite. The odds of that happening are 1 in 700,000!

THERE'S a place called Snake Den Ridge, which connects the Cosby Campground with the Appalachian Trail. It climbs 5.3 miles high into the Great Smokies high elevation peaks. In 1984, just before the connection to the Appalachian Trail, at mile marker number five, an F-4 Phantom slammed nose first into the mountains, causing wreckage to be blown and tossed over nearly twenty acres! There is still wreckage in this area and scattered debris; mainly hikers take some for souvenirs.

IN 1964 A T-28B Marine trainer crashed close to the Blue Ridge Parkway in Nelson County and Augusta County in Virginia, right into the side of the Humpback Mountain. The debris from this crash sits about two hundred yards from the Appalachian Trail, and the tail and other large sections of the plane still lie there.

WHAT IS it that causes twenty million people worldwide to be terrified of flying in an airplane? Aviophobia is the fear of flying in an airplane, the thought of being left free-falling from thirty thousand feet in the air is almost incapacitating, especially to those who fly frequently, even commercially. When you get into an airplane, your fate is no longer in your hands. It's in the hands of the pilot or pilots who are in control of the plane, right? Maybe not.

Approximately eighty-four planes have vanished without a trace since the 1950s when records started being kept. How does that even happen? Even single-engine planes are incredibly large, and most of those that disappeared seemingly into thin air were commercial planes, massive machines gliding gracefully through the air one minute and poof! Gone the next. You're more likely to be killed by a bear in Yellowstone National Park; the odds of that are 1 in 2.1 million. In fact, in the Great Smokies, which is the focus of this information, there's been only one bear attack, ever. In the whole history of this particular national park. So is it really that unlikely there could be some form of portal these planes are accidentally flying into, unable to return?

ON NOVEMBER 24, 1983, a 414 Cessna was flying from West Chicago to the Jackson County airport in the mountains of the Smokies in North Carolina. It crashed at about 6,000 feet at around 6:30 p.m. Inclement weather, poor visibility, and the consumption of alcohol (the pilot's BAL was 0.04%) caused the tragic wreck, where both the pilot and his passenger unfortunately died. There may not have been a flight plan filed, which most likely caused the pilot, who was under the influence and already at a disadvantage, to just be ducking clouds and flying blindly by sight alone. If the plane had been just 150 feet higher in elevation, it would've been able to clear the mountain, and most likely the tragedy would never have occurred. The wreckage still sits after more than thirty-five years. Human error, how do we really know what happened in the final moments and seconds of the occupants' lives, especially in such a relatively small plane? We don't! The fact the pilot had alcohol in his system could be the perfect excuse for some unknown and unseen predator to take action. We would never know.

IN MARCH of 1964 there was a twin-engine Beechcraft that crashed near Parsons Bald in the Great Smoky Mountains, leaving all six people on board tragically deceased. This accident was made even more tragic when a maintenance worker who was part of the rescue team was hiking to the crash site and had a fatal heart attack.

ON DECEMBER 1, 1997, a Cessna 182 went down near Russell Field, the crash killing the only person in the plane, which was the pilot.

ON FEBRUARY 16, 1984, there were seven people aboard a single-engine Cherokee Six airplane when it crashed right onto Mount Buckley. Fortunately all seven occupants survived the crash fairly uninjured.

A CRASH in August of 1956 also left both occupants alive. They were able to walk away from the crash "scratched but unharmed." The crash happened when the pilot power stalled the rented Aeronca trainer into the trees right near Clingmans Dome. The exact location wasn't given, but it was said to have been a valley between Mount Collins and Sweet Ridge at about a four-thousand-foot elevation.

ON FEBRUARY 7, 2021, there was a small plane crash near, of course, the Great Smoky Mountains National Park. Both occupants were pronounced dead at the scene, and the immediate cause of the crash could not be determined. Among the wreckage were the bodies of fifty-eight-year-old Joseph Mackey and seventy-eight-year-old Carl Spray. The Franklin County Sheriff's Office released a statement saying that they would release more information "when appropriate" and did not immediately release any information regarding what had happened and why the plane had crashed. The public is still awaiting more details.

As we read on and on about these crashes, isolated in one general area of the much larger arena of the Great Smoky Mountains and national park, we must keep in mind that the Great Smokies themselves, while absolutely massive in size, are but a speck on the earth when compared to the whole world. So why this site? All of the death, destruction, pain, and chaos in this one localized and general area? Is there something perhaps vampiric, waiting to feed off of all of the devastation?

ON JULY 9, 1964, a United Airlines plane crashed nine miles northeast of Newport, Tennessee, in the

Great Smoky Mountains. According to law enforcement officials, there were no survivors, and only thirty-two of the thirty-nine bodies were able to be recovered in the first few days. The plane was a four-engine Viscount, flight number 823, which originated in Philadelphia and was on its way to Knoxville, Tennessee. A woman who witnessed the crash, a Mrs. Charles Hawk, lives on a farm in the area of the crash and reported seeing the plane suddenly explode in the air. Other witnesses to the tragic and deadly crash reported seeing "bodies flying through the air." The craft was still engulfed in flames when the first police officers showed up. In fact, the craft was so badly charred and damaged that they initially had trouble even determining the name of the airline. Rescue workers said the wreckage was strewn over a half-mile area.

The crash happened at 6:15 eastern time, and the weather was reported to be clear skies. Although there were scattered clouds, there was a four-thousand-foot ceiling and thirty miles of visibility when the plane suddenly and spontaneously combusted. In this case, let's discuss the obvious, where are those other seven bodies? It calls to mind all of the living people, who for whatever reason, maybe hiking or camping, just vanish without a trace with amazing regularity in our national parks and all over the world. The clusters of missing people all over the place, again localized in our national parks. Is this somehow connected to that phenomenon? I mean, how hard is it to find bodies? With all of the hiking and camping and just tourist activity in general every single year, is it really that easy to believe that in 57 YEARS the deceased have never been found? No skulls or bones? Nothing? Maybe one body but seven? Vanished without a trace? Highly improbable! Remember, the odds you'll be poisoned are better than this by a long shot, 1 in 1,400 to be exact.

THE DAY after Christmas in 2016, a small Cessna airplane crashed during its approach to the Gatlinburg-Pigeon Forge airport in Sevierville, Tennessee. The wreckage was located the next day about fifteen miles south-southeast of the airport. A tactical rescue team from the National Park Service had to recover the bodies from the very rugged and rough terrain between Cole Creek and Bear Pen Hollow Branch. The paramedics had to be hoisted down into the crash site, as there was no other way to gain access to it or the people on board. All three occupants, David Starling, the pilot of the small aircraft, his son, Hunter, and his girlfriend, Kim, were deceased. The incredibly rough terrain made it impossible for ground teams to search the area or reach the site. The way the plane was positioned made the rescue mission extremely difficult. It was on a very steep mountainside and posed a potential risk for sliding farther down and causing more damage or possibly even more fatalities. The bodies remained unrecovered until Wednesday, December 28.

While there is no official report as to why the plane went down, it is noted that Starling, while instrument flight rules were in effect, was not IFR rated and had not filed a flight plan. The plane was at 5,400 feet on approach to the airport when contact was last made with the control tower. Starling was flying near Mount Conte, which has an elevation of 6,500 feet

Once again it seems a pilot crashed because he was flying in clouds that were obscuring the mountains.

GREAT SMOKY MOUNTAINS NATIONAL PARK rangers responded to a report of a small plane crash approximately six miles west of Clingmans Dome on April 10, 2020, at approximately 11:00 a.m. The Tennessee Army National Guard had to use a hoist to rescue the pilot of the small plane. They finally reached him and were able to fly him to safety a little under an hour after the crash, near 2 p.m. George Kusterman, the pilot and only occupant of the aircraft, deployed the parachute just north of Silers Bald and Buckeye Gap. At 1:06 p.m. the Tennessee Highway Patrol helicopter located Kusterman, who sustained no injuries and was able to leave the airport he was taken to when rescued, of his own accord and under his own care.

PART 3

———

DISAPPEARANCES

CHAPTER TWENTY-FIVE

THE DENNIS MARTIN DISAPPEARANCE

ONE OF THE most puzzling and disturbing disappearances in the Great Smoky Mountains is that of Dennis Martin. Just six years old when he vanished, Dennis made a huge impression on me. I was just a few months younger than Dennis at the time, and it was my first exposure to the concept of a missing child. It took a bit for me to wrap my five-year-old mind around the event—how could a living, breathing boy, just like me, simply disappear? It can and does happen, and in June of 1969, it did. Dennis Martin walked into the bush of Spence Field and into the pages of history, folklore, and Smoky Mountains mythology.

The story goes that Dennis, his older brother, his father and grandfather had all gone to Cades Cove to spend Father's Day in the beautiful outdoors of the

Great Smokies. The weather in the mountains was exceptionally cool on this particular weekend, a respite from the heat that Dennis, his brother and father had endured at their home an hour and a half or so away in the Bearden neighborhood of Knoxville. Bill Martin, Dennis' father, was a prominent architect at the time in Knoxville, but he enjoyed the trappings of being a family man and father to his two boys. He was anxious on that weekend to pack up the boys, along with their granddad, and spend some quality time in the Great Smokies, a "just the boys outing," if you will.

While they were relaxing after the somewhat rigorous hike up to the Field, the Martin family rested a bit. While they were resting, another family approached. Oddly enough (in one of the many Fortean and/or coincidental facts regarding this case), the other family shared the same last surname—the two Mr. Martins shook hands and agreed that it would be a good idea for the boys from both families to play together while the older gents continued to relax around the campsite.

After about an hour or so, what happened next has been told a couple of different ways—I'm unsure as to which is absolutely correct, so I will err on the side of caution and relate both versions as I heard them. It was said that the boys decided to play a game of hide-and-seek, and that Bill Martin, Dennis' father, observed the younger boy pick a hiding spot behind a clump of bushes. The second version says that the older boys decided to scare the adults and made a plan to walk in a giant circle and come up behind the older men. In this version, Dennis (who was quite a bit younger and small for his age) decided to go in a different direction and meet up with the older lads near the aforementioned clump of bushes. Either way, Bill Martin states that he watched Dennis walk into a clump of brush on that day. It was the last time he would ever see his son.

After the game of hide-and-seek or scare the adults (depending on which version you prefer), Bill Martin noticed that Dennis was no longer with the group. He walked over to the clump of bushes and entered it. Then he walked all the way around it—several times. He questioned the other boys and adults, and all concurred that they had not laid eyes on young Dennis after the games had begun. It was in this moment that Bill realized his son was missing. He instructed Dennis' granddad to hike down to the ranger station while he himself took off in a run down a section of the famous Appalachian Trail that led through the edge of their camping area. This set in motion the greatest manhunt and search and rescue effort the Great Smoky Mountain National Park had ever witnessed. Within two hours, hundreds of park rangers, forestry service employees, and civilian volunteers were combing the hills and woods of Cades Cove, trying to locate the lost boy. As darkness fell, the weather took a turn for the worse (again, an odd coincidence that often happens when people go missing), and torrential rainfalls began. The rain and winds would last several days, severely hampering the search efforts as well as obliterating many clues, such as any footprints Dennis may have left behind.

The FBI was later called in on the case, which is interesting, as the FBI usually does not work missing persons cases unless they feel that a crime has been involved. I will let the reader draw their own conclusions regarding that statement. Furthermore, the details of the case have been denied although multiple Freedom of Information Act documents have been filed.

To make matters even more bizarre, the FBI agent, who was overseeing the case, committed suicide under mysterious circumstances. Whatever information and knowledge he had regarding the Dennis Martin case, he took to the grave with him.

Another family that was visiting Cades Cove that day (but in another area), named the Key family, had ventured to a certain area where a ranger had told them they might be able to spot some of the black bear that are commonly sighted in the mountains. While the family was looking for bear, they heard a blood-curdling scream and then witnessed what they first thought was a bear but later described as a "hairy, rugged man" running uphill away from them through the trees and underbrush. They were not aware of the disappearance until they returned home the next day. When they realized they might have witnessed something in regard to Dennis Martin's mysterious disappearance, they contacted the FBI. Oddly enough, the FBI asked them not to return to Cades Cove to point out the area where the odd sighting took place, but instead offered to meet them in a location that was "halfway for both parties." The agent took their statement, but apparently never shared it with Dennis' father, who was livid when he heard it mentioned on the local news in Knoxville. This began a rift that would forever exist between Bill Martin and the law enforcement agencies working on the case, the FBI in particular. Mr. Martin stated that he felt he had been lied to by the agents and the media and could no longer trust any of them. Through the entire scenario, Bill Martin refused to come off the mountain, spending days and days searching for his young son. As the volunteers swelled, then dwindled as any hope of finding Dennis alive evaporated, the search and rescue effort sadly transformed into a recovery operation.

Sadly, Bill Martin passed away in 2014 (on Halloween, no less), the forty-fifth anniversary of

Dennis' disappearance having happened the previous July. A broken man, Bill rarely spoke with the media and essentially died a broken man—one cannot imagine the mental anguish of enduring over four decades without even a hint of closure.

There are a multitude of programs online on YouTube talking about this very case, and it has been written up in many books. Perhaps the most interesting account is that of ex-law enforcement officer David Paulides in his fascinating tome *Missing 411 - Eastern United States*. I won't go into detail here in regard to Mr. Paulides' findings, but I will state they are very strange, bordering on the bizarre, and well worth the read.

CHAPTER TWENTY-SIX

THE TRENNY GIBSON DISAPPEARANCE

AT THE TIME of her disappearance, Theresa Lynn Trenny Gibson was a sixteen-year-old Bearden High School student from Knoxville, Tennessee, which is, oddly enough, the same city and neighborhood where Dennis Martin lived when he vanished only seven years prior. On October 8, 1976, their science teacher had treated Trenny and her classmates to a surprise field trip.

According to the official story, the students didn't know where they would be going until they were already en route on the bus. After traveling approximately fifty miles to the Great Smoky Mountains National Park, the students had been hiking near both Clingmans Dome, which is the highest point in the Tennessee side of the Smokies, and then followed the Forney Ridge trail to nearby Andrews Bald. Trenny was known to have hiked at least part of the almost two-mile trail with classmate Robert Simpson, who was a friend of Trenny's older brother. Afterwards, other students agreed that the group reached Andrews Bald around 1:30 p.m., and many recalled having seen Trenny and Robert having lunch together.

Being October, it was not only foggy that day in the Smokies, but also on the cold side. Since the trip was a surprise, Trenny wasn't dressed very warmly and ended up borrowing Robert's jacket, which she was apparently still wearing when she disappeared. Robert later stated that he and Trenny did not hike back together, instead having been separated when Robert went off to track a bear, as he put it. Other students on the field trip could remember having seen Trenny amongst the group at approximately 3:00 p.m.

The group at this point headed back toward the parking lot near Clingmans Dome. When the group stopped to take a rest, Trenny continued on alone. Just a few moments later on that fateful fall afternoon would be the last time Trenny Gibson was ever seen. Some of the group claimed to have seen Trenny stop a few dozen yards down the trail and bend down as if she were looking at something off the trail in the woods. Then inexplicably, Trenny stepped off the trail and into the mists of time, never to be seen or heard from again with nary a trace or whisper to be found.

Many theories surfaced afterwards, including that Trenny, soon to be graduating, had instead planned to rendezvous in the parking lot with an older boyfriend, with whom she simply took off, telling no one in the process.

While that theory is interesting, I've always found it implausible, since Trenny did not know until the day of the field trip where her science class would be going. Items found at the spot where Trenny stepped off the trail included three cigarette butts and a partial can of beer. More fresh cigarette butts of the same variety were found at the edge of the roadway, not far from the parking lot. And this was as far as scent dogs would later track Trenny.

Although Robert Simpson was never seriously considered as a suspect, according to authorities, other students claimed that they had spotted Trenny's comb on the dash of his car. Robert was reported to have told Trenny's family that he believed Kelvin Bowman was to blame, as he had once been obsessed with Trenny. Robert further confided to Trenny's sister that if Kelvin had her, he'd kill her. Kelvin was even shot in the foot by Trenny's mother once when he was trying to break into the Gibson residence. Kelvin had spent six months in a youth facility after the incident and was back attending classes at Bearden High School when Trenny disappeared.

Although some students claimed to have seen Kelvin's car shadowing the bus on the field trip, he was cleared after the school principal verified that Kelvin had been at school the entire day.

A few years ago, I mentioned the case to one of my family members in East Tennessee and was shocked to find out she was friends with Trenny's younger sister, Tina. My relative was unaware of all the details of the case and simply knew that Tina's sister had gone missing in the Great Smoky Mountains National Park a few decades ago. I jumped at the chance to talk with Tina, not as an investigator, but rather just as someone who was curious about her sister's disappearance. Tina was friendly and very forthcoming about her knowledge of the case, but sadly didn't have any real earth-shattering information beyond what is already known.

The saddest yet most interesting aspect that I learned from Tina's perspective was how the vanishing of her older sister absolutely devastated her parents and destroyed the home life for the entire family. Tina stated that her parents had always been strict, but after Trenny's disappearance, this increased many-, manyfold.

Her parents' feelings went from sadness and shock

to outright anger and fear, and Trenny's parents each blamed the other and sometimes even Trenny's siblings for the disappearance. The shattered couple eventually went through a bitter divorce. Tina left home as soon as she was eighteen and was basically estranged from the rest of her family. She said that she had always felt that Trenny was miserable with the constrictive home life and simply made her escape at the first opportunity that presented itself.

Tina also stated she wanted to believe that Trenny was alive out there somewhere and enjoying a life of freedom, perhaps in sunny Southern California—but she also said in her heart of hearts, she didn't think Trenny ever left the park alive. Sadly, Tina passed away in 2016 without ever knowing for sure of her older sister's fate, wherever she is. In October of this year (2021), it will be forty-five years since Trenny Gibson walked ahead of her classmates on the trail and simply ceased to exist.

CHAPTER TWENTY-SEVEN

THE THELMA PAULINE "POLLY" MELTON DISAPPEARANCE

YET ANOTHER STRANGE disappearance from within the wilds of the Great Smoky Mountains National Park, this one happened on September 25, 1981, near the Deep Creek Campground on the Deep Creek Trail. Thelma Pauline ("Polly" to her pals and family) was initially hiking with two friends and was last seen at approximately 4:00 p.m. While the trio were hiking, Melton suddenly decided to increase her stride and speed, which caused her to move ahead of her other two hiking companions. The two ladies observed her crest a small hill on the trail and move out of their view on the other side. It was the last time Polly Melton would ever be seen.

Polly's two hiking buddies, who knew her quite well, assumed that she had gone back to the Deep Creek

Campground, where she and her husband had their Airstream trailer set up in a rented space. When the other two ladies finished their hike and arrived back at Deep Creek Campground at around 4:30 p.m., they were surprised to find no sign of Polly having returned. Polly's husband was still inside the Airstream, where he had remained while Polly and the other ladies had gone on their short hike. When asked, Mr. Melton stated that he had not seen nor heard from Polly since the ladies had left in a group earlier in the afternoon.

Polly's husband officially reported her as a missing person to a park ranger at about 6:00 p.m., approximately two hours after her hiking partners had seen her disappear from view ahead of them on the trail. Her husband further stated that Polly was very well acquainted with the Deep Creek Trail, which runs parallel with Deep Creek in the park, and from which the campground also takes its name. There was nothing found to indicate that Polly had ventured off the trail, nor was there any indication of an abduction or any sign of a struggle or any reason to suspect foul play in the area of the trail where Polly was last spotted.

The only thing her husband noticed to be missing from the Airstream trailer was Polly's cigarettes, although the other ladies she was hiking with were fairly certain that she was carrying her cigarettes and lighter with her on the trail hike when she disappeared.

Also, as far as the husband could remember, Polly had apparently seemed to follow what was her normal routine throughout the day prior to her vanishing, the sole notable exception being that Polly chose not to volunteer at a local senior citizens' center, where she helped serve meals to the elderly patrons. Although she usually volunteered at the senior citizens' center every day, she had—for unknown reasons—chosen not to attend on the day of her disappearance.

Other than apparently her cigarettes and lighter, Polly was not carrying anything else with her—she had no money, no identification cards, nor any of her prescription medications with her when she vanished into thin air. Nor did she have any keys with her, as her doctor had not permitted her to drive at the time due to underlying medical conditions. Her husband was said to have had the keys to their Airstream trailer in his pocket at the time of her disappearance.

As far as her husband or friends know, Polly was not entertaining any suicidal thoughts at the time of her disappearance, although it was reported that she had been under a doctor's care recently for minor depression, but was not considered a danger to herself or others, certainly.

Polly was known to have been a heavy user of Valium (for its sedation and calming effects) as recently as 1979, a full two years before she vanished in the mountains. Although it was assumed that Polly had long since given up her need for Valium when she went missing in 1981, her husband noted that his prescription of Valium appeared to have gone missing at approximately the same time as his wife vanished. It is not believed that Polly took her husband's medication bottle with her, though, as she left behind her own necessary prescription medicine bottles.

After her disappearance, Polly's church pastor came forward and stated that she had confessed to him that she was grieving over the recent death of her mother, shortly before the time she vanished. The pastor, although he had no evidence to back up the claim, also stated that he believed Polly may have been involved in an extramarital affair behind her husband's back at the time of the disappearance, but again, this is only speculation on the pastor's part. Oddly enough (perhaps supporting the pastor's theory), Polly's supervisor at the senior citizens' center where she was a daily volunteer later told authorities that although Polly had never been observed to use the facility's telephone, she had, indeed, placed a telephone call to an unknown party on the day before she went missing. It is unknown, however, if the call that Polly placed from the senior citizens' center was in any way related to her subsequent vanishing act .

As far as is known, Polly Melton has not been seen or heard from since that fateful fall afternoon in September 1981. As of this writing, in early September of 2020, Thelma Pauline "Polly" Melton's disappearance remains unsolved.

CHAPTER TWENTY-EIGHT

THE DEREK JOSEPH LUEKING DISAPPEARANCE

WHILE MOST OF the infamous cases of missing people in the Great Smoky Mountains National Park are from the twentieth century, one of the more disturbing disappearances is a mystery for the twenty-first century. One Derek Joseph Lueking, of Louisville, Tennessee, left the Microtel where he had spent the night in Cherokee, North Carolina, at 4 a.m. the morning of Saturday, March 17, 2012. Lueking was last observed alone on the hotel surveillance cameras, carrying a small backpack.

Derek was twenty-four years old at the time and, although depressed over the recent loss of his grandfather, was not known to be suicidal. His father states that once they gained entrance to the room where Derek had previously spent the night, there was a Bible on the bed and a partially consumed bottle of liquor on the floor. Derek wasn't known to be a drinker, and his father says the way the items were laid out, it looked as if Derek was torn with making a choice.

Derek's automobile was spotted the same morning at approximately 8:30 a.m. at Newfound Gap in the Smoky Mountains. A note containing the cryptic and mysterious phrase "Don't Look For Me" was found inside his car along with Derek's wallet and the key to the car. The cryptic message on the note was not addressed to anyone in particular, and even Derek's distraught family thought it could have been left for park service employees so they wouldn't tow his car away in his absence, as if he was planning to be away from the vehicle for an extended period of time. His family also revealed that Derek was a fan and follower of extreme outdoorsman Bear Grylls and most likely had enough survival skills and equipment to endure a long stay in the wilds of the Great Smokies—however, Derek did not take very much of the thousand-plus dollars of equipment or supplies he had recently purchased with him when he left his car.

According to a statement made by Derek's father, the family believe the only things he took with him were: "... at least a backpack, a waterproof watch, a Bear Grylls survival tool pack (including a multi-tool, a small flashlight, and a fire starter rod), a Gerber pack axe, several pages of a military survival manual, a knife sharpener, a compass/thermometer, one hundred feet of black parachute cord, a head lamp, a pocketknife, an iPod Touch, and some granola bars..."

Perhaps the oddest thing about the disappearance is that no one is certain Derek even entered the park on that day, meaning he may have gone missing in the parking area—thus having vanished before he even set foot in the actual park—a first for the missing person cases of the Great Smoky Mountains National Park. Even though park service employees state that the Newfound Gap area was "even busier than usual" that fateful spring day, not one person in the park—park employee, hiker, tourist, ranger or otherwise—could recall seeing Derek, despite the thousands of fliers that were tacked up and passed out to hikers traveling in both directions. Even the park service admits that it would be "highly unusual" for *someone* not to have at least passed Derek on the hiking trails.

Despite extensive search and rescue efforts, no trace of Derek has ever been found. On a Facebook page titled "Find Derek Lueking" (which is maintained and monitored by the family), this message is listed even though the young man has been missing a little over nine years (as of this writing):

"There is still the possibility that Derek Lueking is not in the park, and we would like to make sure the information is out there so people can look for Derek out in the world. We have not given up hope on finding Derek and are doing everything in our power to work with and help the rangers who are investigating as well as trying to make sure the information is out in the world as well."

CHAPTER TWENTY-NINE

THE GHOST OF LITTLE EDD, THE WANDERING BOY

THE YEAR WAS 1915, and a feisty twelve-year-old boy had just had a terrible fight with his father. Angry, and perhaps a little stubborn as well, the boy left his home in Blount County, Tennessee, (near Maryville) determination etched on his face—he would show his father—he would walk all the way to his grandparents' house... even though his grandparents lived all the way on the other side of the Great Smoky Mountains, in North Carolina.

Wandering along what is now US Highway 441 through the Great Smoky Mountains National Park (but was then little more than a deeply rutted wagon trail), the boy pushed onward through the mountains. Shortly, he reached the summit at Indian Gap and then began the long, slow descent into Western North Carolina.

Somewhere along the way, the snow began to fall—it was almost springtime in the Smokies, being late march, but old man winter is still known to blow a chill in the higher elevations of the rugged mountains, sometimes well into April.

The boy considered himself tough and knowledgeable of wood lore—but he hadn't counted on a freak snowstorm blowing in while on his trek. By the time he tried to find somewhere to seek refuge for the night, it was too late. Tired, the boy lay down underneath a craggy rock overhang, very near where the Appalachian Trail passes through the national park, and went to sleep. He never awakened, having frozen to death in the below-freezing temperatures of the howling mountain wind and wet, heavy snowfall.

Some time later, after the snow had passed, a group of hunters found the boy's body underneath the overhang and carried him all the way back down to what was then the Sugarlands area of the Great Smoky Mountains National Park. Unknown to anyone in the area and carrying nothing that could identify him, the boy was placed in a simple unmarked grave. And there he remained, unknown, unnamed, and unclaimed, for over sixty years.

Thanks to a retired National Park Service ranger, the mystery of the wandering boy was solved. Having led many campers along the Old Sugarlands Trail, Ranger Butch McDade knew the story of how the boy was found by heart—but what neither he nor anyone else knew was who the boy was, where he came from, and how he ended up frozen to death in the wilderness at the tender age of twelve, with no one ever coming forth to claim the body.

A simple blank slab was later placed to mark the grave where the boy was buried in 1915—but now, thanks to the diligence of Ranger McDade and something short of a miracle, another headstone has been added. It bears the name "Edd McKinley."

In 2009, Park Ranger Butch McDade retired from the National Park Service after serving five years in the Great Smoky Mountains National Park.

Over the years, Butch has spent many hours conducting extensive research on the mystery of Edd McKinley, the wandering boy.

Butch states that unlike the case of Dennis Martin— the six-year-old who famously disappeared from Spence Field in 1969 while on a family picnic, which is discussed in greater detail elsewhere in this book—the family and relatives of little Edd McKinley passed away with at least some closure in knowing the fate of the poor, long-lost boy.

"The beauty of this story," Butch say, "as opposed to

other mysteries of people vanishing in the Smokies, is that this brought closure, at least for some family members," McDade said. "It's a compelling human interest story with a nice ending."

It was through the process of this extensive research that Butch McDade eventually uncovered a series of strange, almost Fortean coincidences that led to the eventual positive identification of it being Edd's remains as those that occupied the sad, unmarked grave. One of Butch's greatest assets and a valuable source of key information was a man by the name of Glenn Cardwell. Cardwell was raised on a farm inside what is today the national park, and had also spent thirty-four years serving as a park ranger in the Great Smokies.

At one time Cardwell was even the mayor of the town of Pittman Center, just east of the city of Gatlinburg. He was still in office well into his eighties—at that time the oldest serving mayor in the state of Tennessee—and was for years the oldest living link to the tragic story of Little Edd.

Way back in May of 1975, Cardwell was temporarily assigned to the Sugarlands Visitor Center. One afternoon, an elderly lady by the name of Virgie Smith, from the nearby city of Knoxville, Tennessee, came in and told the sad story of her brother who had run away from home in 1915 and was never seen or heard of again.

She had inquired at the reception desk where she might begin to look for any information someone at the park might have, by chance. The young girl park volunteer who was at the desk pointed to Glenn Cardwell, who just so happened to be in the visitor center that day and said that if anyone here would know anything about it, it would be him.

Cardwell made his way over to the reception desk and listened intently as Smith tearfully described her family's years of attempts to find the truth and to bring closure to her young brother's disappearance.

Virgie's impassioned plea jogged Cardwell's mind, and he recalled a handwritten letter that he'd had on file for years. The letter was from none other than Gatlinburg resident Lucinda Ogle, daughter of legendary mountain storyteller and guide Wiley Oakley. Lucinda Ogle, being a member of one of the area's founding families, had a very keen interest in the stories and folklore of the national park and had written Cardwell a note in regard to a news article she'd heard recently (at that time) about a search and rescue effort in the Great Smokies for another lost little boy.

In the letter she had written, Lucinda Ogle made a casual reference to a memory she had of the tale of an unidentified boy whose body had been brought to the Sugarlands community in the early 1900s. He had been found frozen to death beneath a rock overhang a short distance away from what is known today as the Appalachian Trail.

Glenn Cardwell picked up the phone at the reception desk and called Lucinda Ogle directly, gave a brief explanation for the call, and handed the phone over to Virgie Smith. When Smith realized that what Lucinda Ogle began telling her was most likely a firsthand account of what had become of her long-lost brother after all these years, Virgie Smith openly wept.

Looking back, Cardwell has often said that this very moment was the absolute pinnacle of his career with the National Park Service.

"I give thanks to God I just happened to be at the visitors center that day," he was later quoted as saying.

Cardwell decided he would take Smith to visit Lucinda Ogle at her home to hear the entire story in person, so they left the Sugarlands visitor center together.

At Ogle's home, Virgie Smith learned that her runaway brother had been found by a pair of men as they returned from a hunting trip. Upon discovering his cold, lifeless body, they carried him the rest of the way to the Sugarlands community in order to have the body claimed. However, they had no luck, and no one stepped forward to claim or identify the body.

The good people of the Sugarlands community waited a few days, and when the body still hadn't been claimed, they decided to proceed with a burial for the poor little boy.

Little Edd was dressed in a crisp white shirt and a pair of overalls, and he was laid to rest in a cleared corner on the hillside. They felt the least they could do was to give him some fresh clothes and a proper Christian burial. Every resident of the Sugarlands community came to pay their respects to the unknown boy, and it's said that so many flowers were brought by them that Little Edd's grave was the most decorated in the graveyard.

Since the death appeared to be accidental, there was no official investigation by the authorities.

Although the details and dates made Virgie Smith sure this had been her brother, it was one detail from Lucinda Ogle that convinced her this was, indeed, her long-lost sibling.

Upon hearing from Lucinda's brother Earnest Ogle (who had been ten years old at the time and had even help dig the lost boy's grave) that the boy had red hair, it left Virgie absolutely convinced... Her brother, Edd

McKinley, had been a redhead as well. Virgie once again broke down in tears.

About six months later, in September of 1975, a small group drove up the old road, now referred to as the Old Sugarland Trail, to the quiet mountain graveyard. The small group of mourners included Virgie Smith, her son Don, and the Ogles.

Proudly leading the somber procession was none other than Park Ranger Glenn Cardwell. The group had with them a recently carved marble slab bearing little Edd McKinley's name and the dates of his birth and death. The headstone was small but impressive and weighed close to two hundred pounds.

Don Smith, Edd McKinley's nephew, helped lift the slab onto the burial site, where it was carefully laid at the foot of the plain piece of fieldstone that had served to mark the final resting place of the unknown wandering boy's final resting place for the last sixty years or so.

"Mrs. Smith wanted to make one last stab at solving her brother's mystery before she died, " Butch McDade stated. "She wanted to tie up loose ends. I'm sure she had been a searcher all her life."

And now the ghost of Little Edd McKinley, the wandering boy of the Smoky Mountains, rests peacefully.

IN CLOSING

Well, there you have it. The Great Smoky Mountains National Park is many things... expansive, beautiful, and popular with tourists (it's the most visited national park in the country)... Yet also frightening, dangerous, and downright deadly to those unfortunate enough to be in the wrong place at the wrong time.

With all that has been said, I truly do not wish to discourage anyone from visiting this strange and wonderful place. Just keep these stories in mind, stay safe, stay alive, and come back with a camera full of pictures, a head full of strange and beautiful encounters, and feel proud that you lived to tell the tale.

Thank you for reading this book, and I look forward to telling more tales of other national parks—many of which are just as weird and fascinating. In the meantime, be good to yourselves and each other, and I'll talk to you next time. Be well and be blessed.

—Steve

Volume 2
National Park Mysteries & Disappearances
California (Yosemite, Joshua Tree, Mount Shasta)
Now Available

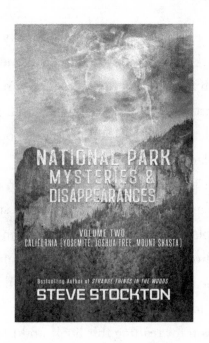

ABOUT THE AUTHOR

Steve Stockton grew up in the wilds of East Tennessee, but now makes his home in the Pacific Northwest, where he enjoys finding all kinds of new, weird places to seek out. As well as the great outdoors, he also enjoys hearing from his readers.

If you have a story you'd like to share for future volumes or would just like to say hello, you can reach him at SteveStockton81@Gmail.com

facebook.com/steve.stockton81
twitter.com/strangeandodd

ALSO BY STEVE STOCKTON

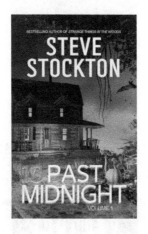

13 PAST MIDNIGHT SERIES

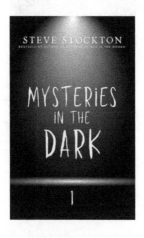

MYSTERIES IN THE DARK SERIES

STRANGE THINGS IN THE WOODS

MY STRANGE WORLD

Printed in the USA
CPSIA information can be obtained
at www.ICGtesting.com
LVHW041559031223
765583LV00038B/755

9 781954 528062